D0301689

UNIVERSITY LIBRARY

Lifelong Learning and the University

Lifelong Learning and the University:
A Post-Dearing Agenda

David Watson and
Richard Taylor

UK   The Falmer Press, 1 Gunpowder Square, London, EC4A 3DE
USA The Falmer Press, Taylor & Francis Inc., 1900 Frost Road, Suite 101, Bristol, PA 19007

© D. Watson and R. Taylor, 1998

All rights reserved. No part of this publication may be reproduced, stored in a retrieval system, or transmitted in any form or by any means, electronic, mechanical, photocopying, recording or otherwise, without permission in writing from the Publisher.

First published in 1998

A Catalogue record for this book is available from the British Library

Library of Congress Cataloging-in-Publication Data are available on request

ISBN 0 7507 0785 2 cased
ISBN 0 7507 0784 4 paper

Jacket design by Caroline Archer

Typeset in 10/12pt Garamond by
Graphicraft Typesetters Ltd., Hong Kong.

Printed in Great Britain by Biddles Ltd, Guildford and King's Lynn on paper which has a specified pH value on final paper manufacture of not less than 7.5 and is therefore 'acid free'.

Every effort has been made to contact copyright holders for their permission to reprint material in this book. The publishers would be grateful to hear from any copyright holder who is not here acknowledged and will undertake to rectify any errors or omissions in future editions of this book.

Contents

List of Figures

5 Getting on in Higher Education

7 Modules, Semesters and Credits

10 The Professional Dimension

11 Quality and Standards

12 Supporting Students

13 Supporting Institutions

14 Supporting Staff

20 The Dearing Vision: A Prognosis

List of Acronyms

AGCAS	Association of Graduate Careers Advisory Services
AGR	Association of Graduate Recruiters
APL	Accreditation of Prior Learning
APEL	Accreditation of Prior Experiential Learning
APR	Age Participation Rate
AUT	Association of University Teachers
BTEC	Business and Technician Education Council
CAT	Colleges of Advanced Technology
CATS	Credit Accumulation and Transfer Scheme
CBI	Confederation of British Industry
CE	Continuing Education
CIHE	Council for Industry and Higher Education
C&IT	Communications and Information Technology
CNAA	Council for National Academic Awards
CPD	Continuing Professional Development
CVCP	Committee of Vice-Chancellors and Principals
CVE	Continuing Vocational Education
DES	Department of Education and Science
DfEE	Department for Education and Employment
DL	Distance Learning
EU	European Union
EYLL	European Year of Lifelong Learning
FE	Further Education
FEIs	Further Education Institutions
GDP	Gross Domestic Product
GNP	Gross National Product
GNVQ	General National Vocational Qualification
GSP	Graduate Standards Programme
HE	Higher Education
HEQC	Higher Education Quality Council
HEFCE	Higher Education Funding Council for England
HEIs	Higher Education Institutions
HESA	Higher Education Statistics Agency
HMI	Her Majesty's Inspectorate
HNC	Higher National Certificate
HND	Higher National Diploma
JANET	Joint Academic Network

JISC	Joint Information Systems Committee
LEA	Local Education Authority
NAB	National Advisory Body
NCE	National Commission on Education
NCIHE	National Committee of Inquiry into Higher Education
NCF	National Credit Framework
NCVQ	National Council for Vocational Qualifications
NETTs	National Education and Training Targets
NIACE	National Institute of Adult and Continuing Education
NUM	National Union of Miners
NUS	National Union of Students
NVQ	National Vocational Qualification
OECD	Organization for Economic Cooperation and Development
OFSTED	Office for Standards in Education
PAMs	Professions Allied to Medicine
PCET	Post-Compulsory Education and Training
PCFC	Polytechnics and Colleges Funding Council
PFI	Private Finance Initiative
QA	Quality Assurance
QAA	Quality Assurance Agency
RAE	Research Assessment Exercise
RB	Responsible Body
SARTOR	Standards and Routes to Registration
SCOP	Standing Conference of Principals
SCOTVEC	Scottish Vocational Education Council
SEDA	Staff and Educational Developmental Association
SMEs	Small and Medium-sized Enterprises
TECs	Training and Enterprise Councils
TGWU	Transport and General Workers Union
TUC	Trades Union Congress
UACE	Universities' Association for Continuing Education
UCAS	Universities and Colleges Admissions Service
UCOSDA	Universities' and Colleges' Staff Development Agency
UFC	Universities Funding Council
UGC	University Grants Committee
WBL	Work-Based Learning
WEA	Workers Educational Association

Foreword

Professor Martin Harris

The CVCP has published its considered response to the Dearing Report in *A New Partnership: Universities, Students, Business and the Nation* (CVCP, 1997e). Like David Watson and Richard Taylor, I feel that the controversies that led up to the National Committee of Inquiry, the Report itself, and a range of positive reactions to it (including from the CVCP) have inspired a powerful sense of potential renewal. But, like them, I also know that all of the main partners in the higher education enterprise have to play their parts if this sense of renewal is not to be dissipated and replaced by cynicism or (even worse) indifference.

The main contribution of their work is that it takes the key issues — of changes in society, culture and work, of national needs (for high quality education throughout life as well as creative and effective research), of government policy (not least on funding), and of changes in the contemporary map of knowledge — and draws them into the everyday life of universities and colleges. In different ways higher education has always been engaged with such issues, but often slowly, selectively, and until recently almost always on its own terms. Watson and Taylor show how aspects of this response, and elements of the corresponding internal culture of universities themselves, will have to change in order for higher education to play its full part in the learning society.

They are equally strong on aspects of university life in which both continuity and restoration are vital. The autonomy of institutions and the freedom of individual thinkers have between them given great service to a society needing special places for reflection and fundamental research. These places, and the circumstances that enable them to thrive, must be maintained. The authors are fully committed to this proposition, but also demonstrate how access to and participation in the dialogue which is at the heart of higher education can, and should, be extended and made more democratic. In this sense the call by the Universities Association for Continuing Education (UACE), for CE genuinely to be in the mainstream, is persuasive.

Finally, they have provided the added bonus of offering a detailed, early analysis of the impact of the specific recommendations in the Dearing Report on lifelong learning in and through higher education. Like the CVCP, they have misgivings about the strength of the new arrangements for part-time students and the detail of proposals for further support from business. Also like the CVCP they find the majority of the recommendations running with the grain of best practice and historical commitments within the sector. Their chief worries, like ours, are about the availability and the application of funding. If Dearing, and the response to his report by New Labour, can put that right, there is in this book a mature and valuable guide to the prospects for lifelong learning within our universities.

Martin Harris
Vice-Chancellor of the University of Manchester
and Chairman of the Committee of Vice-Chancellors and Principals
November 1997

Introduction

The Report of the National Committee of Inquiry into Higher Education chaired by Sir Ron Dearing was published in July 1997 (NCIHE, 1997). It represents the first officially-sponsored systematic examination of the United Kingdom's system of higher education since the Robbins Report, now over a third of a century old (Robbins, 1963). Like Robbins, Dearing was charged with not only making recommendations about contemporary issues and problems, but also with looking reasonably far ahead, in his case for at least 20 years.

The vision that has emerged is not just about higher education, but about the role of a total national educational system in supporting and enriching a society and an economy. The role of universities and colleges is seen embedded in a world of compulsory education, of professional and vocational learning throughout life, and of use of educational resources for personal development; in other words of a learning society.

The immediate impetus for the Dearing Inquiry was the financial crisis in higher education of the early 1990s brought about by the cumulative effects of under-funded expansion. Its timing, terms of reference and membership were agreed by the major political parties as a short-term and uncharacteristic act of collusion to keep the issue of potential student contributions to fees and maintenance (perceived, perhaps short-sightedly, as a middle-class vote loser) off the agenda for the 1997 General Election.

The effectiveness (and persuasiveness) of the Committee's recommendations in alleviating some of these shorter term problems is being tested at the time of writing. This book is not a direct contribution to the resolution of such questions; nor is it a further historical and analytical attempt at explanation of how the crisis of the early 1990s arose. Rather, like the Committee itself, the authors have sought to take a longer and more holistic view; to consider the underlying implications of genuine lifelong learning for the university system, and how institutions and the system as a whole will need to adjust to realize its full potential. We have three main goals: to describe what a UK higher education system that is genuinely part of a national learning society might look like, and the impetus this should provide to radical reform; to identify features of its historical (especially recent) development, as well as the wider social factors, which might inhibit or encourage its performance in this way; and to assess the coherence, desirability and practicality of the Dearing proposals in bringing about this end.

Our intended audience is also threefold: people within institutions who have it within their control to accelerate desirable change (not only institutional managers, but also course leaders, research leaders, lecturers and support staff with substantial influence over course design); people outside higher education who, as significant stake-holders, ought to have a keen interest in these developments (politicians, employers, those working at other levels within the education system and in other public services); and general readers interested in an early assessment of the impact of the Dearing proposals.

The structure of what follows is designed to expose the lack of fit between traditional higher education and the world of lifelong learning, and to lay out the practical challenges to the university, as well as some of the political issues for a wider society, in bringing about the desired convergence. In this process we believe in a mixture of incremental and radical change, the former keeping faith with the historical commitments of the university system — to openness, to mutual assurance of standards and quality, and to pursuing uncomfortable ideas wherever they may lead — and the latter involving significant innovation in teaching and learning methods and styles, in responsiveness to various client groups, amounting in some ways to a new compact between universities, civil society and the state.

The recent dramatic expansion of higher education, like the expansion after Robbins, has raised questions about both the nature and the structure of the system. Unlike that earlier expansion, which was relatively generously funded from public sources, it has been significantly and damagingly under-funded. Moreover, in practice Robbins perpetuated a system with an essentially elite structure, recruitment and culture, based around full-time study (usually away from home) for 18–21-year-olds. The country now faces the prospects of a genuinely mass system of HE, with the potential to develop in both more democratic and more socially responsive directions. Like Dearing, we see the concept of lifelong learning at the heart of this approach.

In terms of what follows in the bulk of the text, a section setting the scene in terms of changes between Robbins and Dearing (Part 1) is followed in turn by analyses of the actual and potential systems measured in terms of patterns of participation (Part 2), the curriculum and its delivery (Part 3), the resources made available and under what conditions (Part 4). Part 5 then turns from internal development to the question of the impact of the system in terms of work and the economy, culture and social cohesion, and community development (including the university itself as a community). Finally (Part 6), we offer a tentative prognosis of the chances of the Dearing vision of a higher education contributing to the learning society. In each section we identify the relevant specific recommendations in the Dearing Report (of which there are 93 in total) and their prospects for practical success.

We do not wish to discourage readers from tackling the full Dearing Report and the associated evidence published with it, which goes into greater depth, and at greater length, than much of the analysis offered here. Rather we have viewed Dearing as a contribution to policy (at various levels from central government to individual institutions) and attempted to assess the impact of that policy.

A final introductory word is in order about our personal perspectives on these questions. We are both elected officers of the sector-wide group — the Universities Association for Continuing Education (UACE) — that has perhaps pressed most consistently from within the system for it to adapt fully to the lifelong learning agenda. One of us has worked for all of his career within the 'traditional' university sector, the other similarly within the previously-termed 'public' or 'new university' sector. During our nearly four years in office we have learned considerably from each other. One of us was a member of the Dearing Committee itself. We have been helped enormously in putting this account together by a variety of colleagues and helpful critics, notably Rachel Bowden of the University of Brighton Education Research Centre whose contribution both to the evidential basis of our arguments and the coherence of the book as a whole has been invaluable. Denise Johnson also worked quickly and accurately in preparing the text. Special thanks are due to our colleagues in UACE, to Stuart Laing, Betty Skolnick, Linda Miles and Rob Humphreys, and to the students who allowed their stories to be included in chapter 6. The errors and the prejudices which survive in what follows are, however, unquestionably our own.

David Watson
Richard Taylor
October 1997

Part 1

The Context: From Robbins to Dearing

1   Changes in UK Higher Education

It has become fashionable to describe UK higher education as having shifted over the past decade from an 'elite' to a 'mass' system. It has certainly grown, when measured by the number of students, the number of institutions concerned, and the level of personal and social investment. But this growth has been neither steady nor straightforward.

From Robbins to Baker: University Demography

Looking back over the numbers of students involved in higher education during the last half century, we can safely identify three periods wherein numbers interacted with policy objectives to produce a distinct atmosphere or culture within HE: pre-Robbins, post-Robbins and post-Baker. The latter two phases were characterized by distinct spurts of growth, followed by governmental second thoughts. Looking further inside the institutions — checking out the demographic features of participation — it is clear, however, that the kind of qualitative changes that most commentators would associate with 'mass' higher education have still to be fully achieved. What two Conservative Secretaries of State, the Kenneths (Baker and Clarke) have achieved is really, as described by the former Universities Association for Continuing Education (UACE) Vice-chairman David Robertson, a 'crowded traditional system'.

Figures 1.1 and 1.2 below show what has happened nationally to the number of students in higher education between 1960 and 1996 and to the age participation rate (APR).

This growth can be differentiated by both mode and level of study. From the perspective of lifelong learning two developments are of special significance here: the steady growth of part-time undergraduate numbers in spite of their unfavourable treatment in the system of public support (see chapter 12), and the huge expansion of postgraduate study, on 'taught' rather than 'research' programmes.

Simultaneously the demographic characteristics of the participants in higher education have changed over the period.

Figure 1.4 shows the gender breakdown since 1979.

Figure 1.5 focuses on age, and the rate of mature participation.

Figure 1.6, regrettably over a narrower period as a result of inadequate data, shows what we know of the class basis of participation. Influential studies, such as that by A.H. Halsey for the National Commission on Education

Figure 1.1   Total HE students UK, 1960/61 to 1995/96

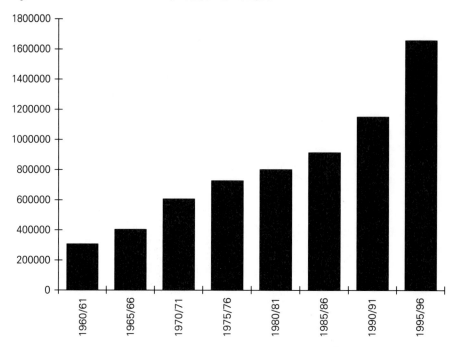

Source: DES, 1967; QSC, 1995.

Figure 1.2   Higher education age participation index (API) — GB institutions, 1961–95

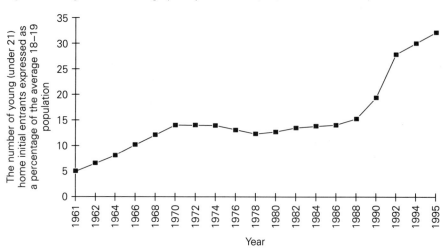

Note: Due to minor changes in definition, the years 1961 to 1970 inclusive are not strictly comparable with later years, and the years from 1980 onwards are not strictly comparable with earlier years.
Source: NCIHE, 1997, Chart 3.5.

Figure 1.3   Number of students by mode of study and level of course, 1979–96

Sources: DES, 1991, 1992; DfE, 1994; IES, 1996; HESA, 1996, 1997.

Legend:
- PT Postgraduate
- FT Postgraduate
- PT Other Undergraduate
- PT First Degree
- FT Other Undergraduate
- FT First Degree

Figure 1.4   Women as a percentage of total home full-time students, 1979–96
(Great Britain)

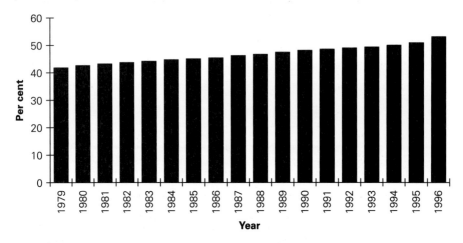

Sources: DES, 1991, 1992; DfE, 1994; HESA, 1996, 1997; IES, 1996

Figure 1.5   Percentage of home full-time first year students on undergraduate courses
aged 21 and over and, 25 and over, 1979–96 (Great Britain)

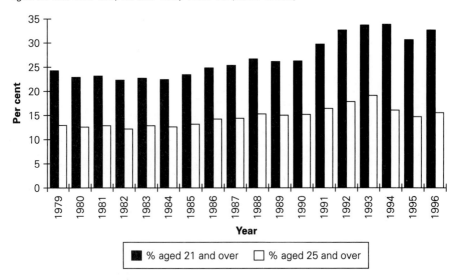

Sources: DES, 1991, 1992; DfE, 1994; HESA, 1996, 1997; IES, 1996.

(NCE), show that throughout both spurts of growth and 'consolidation' (post-Robbins and post-Baker) the proportion of entrants from working-class families has remained inexorably the same, although their absolute numbers have been allowed to grow. We return to this issue about equity, and the relationship of 'fairness' to expansion in chapter 4.

Figure 1.6   Participation rates for Great Britain, by social class, 1991–96

Academic Year	1991/92	1992/93	1993/94	1994/95	1995/96
I — Professional (A)	55%	71%	73%	78%	79%
II — Intermediate (B)	36%	39%	42%	45%	45%
IIIn — Skilled non-manual (C1)	22%	27%	29%	31%	31%
IIIm — Skilled manual (C2)	11%	15%	17%	18%	18%
IV — Partly skilled (D)	12%	14%	16%	17%	17%
V — Unskilled (E)	6%	9%	11%	11%	12%
Total	23%	28%	30%	32%	32%

Note: Participation rates calculated as the number of young (aged less than 21) initial entrants expressed as a proportion of the average 18 to 19-year-old GB population. The 'spurt' between 1991 and 1992 is partly explained by the impact of the 1992 census.
Source: DfEE,1997c.

Figure 1.7   Ethnicity in higher education and the national population, 1994, per cent

Ethnic Group	18–20 years		21–27 years		28–37 years		38–47 years		48 years and over	
White	87.8	(92.7)	83.5	(93.1)	86.4	(93.1)	91.8	(94.8)	93.1	(97.3)
Black	1.7	(1.8)	5.8	(2.1)	7.7	(2.5)	3.7	(1.2)	2.8	(0.9)
Indian	4.5	(2.0)	3.6	(1.8)	1.4	(1.8)	0.9	(1.8)	1.1	(0.8)
Pakistani	2.0	(1.4)	2.4	(1.1)	0.6	(0.8)	0.4	(0.7)	0.3	(0.3)
Other	4.0	(2.1)	4.6	(1.8)	3.9	(1.8)	3.3	(1.5)	2.7	(0.6)
All	100	(100)	100	(100)	100	(100)	100	(100)	100	(100)

Note: Numbers in parentheses show the figures for the UK population as a whole.
Source: NCIHE, 1997, Table 7.4.

On ethnicity, much of the useful recent work lacks the time series that would enable us to draw dynamic conclusions (Modood and Shiner, 1994). Figure 1.7 shows the position in 1994–95.

Finally, figure 1.8 provides no more than the base data for what will have to be a key consideration of future evaluation of participation rates following the Disability Discrimination Act of 1997. One of the Dearing Committee's powerful but informal recommendations is that 'over the long term institutions', which are currently exempt, should 'seek to honour the spirit of the DDA' (NCIHE, 1997, Main Report 7.42).

Figure 1.8   Numbers of UK domiciled undergraduate students by disability, 1994

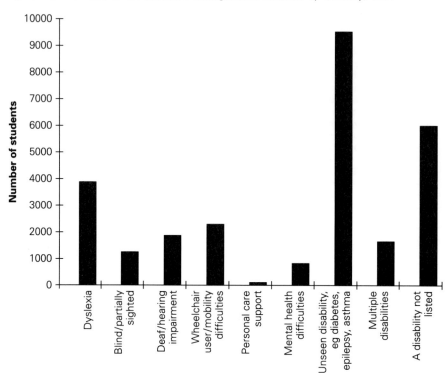

Note: Nearly 27,000 undergraduate students are known to have a disability, about 2 per cent of the total student body. It is estimated that in the population at large 7 per cent of 18–30-year-olds have some type of disability.
Source: HEFCE, 1996a.

Collectively this data raises questions about the relationship of qualitative and quantitative characteristics. It is, however, salutary to take a couple of snapshots in time to compare the key features of participation in the post-Robbins and post-Baker systems at their height (in 1979 and 1992), before two Conservative Secretaries of State (Keith Joseph and John Patten) declared that enough was enough and sought to retrench or 'consolidate' the system.

One perhaps controversial conclusion is that Robbins prompted certain basic qualitative changes in the system (as discussed in Part 3) while the Baker/Clarke effect has been chiefly quantitative. Certainly there have been much greater changes in the patterns of participation than in the higher education product itself as a result of the Conservative stewardship between 1979 and 1997.

Where the Conservative government did, however, make a profound difference was in arrangements for funding, for governance and for overall direction of the system.

Figure 1.9 Aspects of participation post-Robbins and post-Baker

	Post-Robbins 1979	Post-Baker 1992
Age Participation Index (API)	12.4%	27.8%
Percentage of first year home full-time students on undergraduate courses aged 21 or more	24.0%	33.0%
Women as a percentage of all first-year full-time students	40.8%	47.3%
Social Class: Clerical and working	37% (1978)	42% (1993)

Sources: DES, 1991; DfE, 1994; Smithers and Robinson, 1995.

From Robbins to Baker: The Planning and Policy Framework

The Conservative government of 1979–97 inherited two national systems of higher education: a 'university system' as substantially modified by Robbins; and a polytechnic and college sector (often referred to as the 'public sector', formally in local government control but with a strong national dimension as envisaged by Labour Secretary of State Tony Crosland in his famous 'Woolwich' speech) (Crosland, 1965). From these, in a series of bold (some said foolhardy) steps they created either one or three systems, depending on the interpretation of the emergence of the funding councils.

The speed of change was certainly remarkable, and seemed to have much to do with the temperaments of successive Secretaries of State. These alternated between 'consolidators' (Mark Carlisle, John MacGregor, and Gillian Shephard) and 'activists' like Keith Joseph (who attempted both to levy tuition fees and to squeeze the size of the university system, and hence caused middle-class outrage in the early 1980s), Kenneth Baker (author of the so-called Great Educational Reform Bill of 1988) and Kenneth Clarke (creator of the 'new' university system and unitary funding with the 1992 Further and Higher Education Act). The 1988 Act wound up the Universities Grants Committee (UGC), creating the Universities Funding Council (UFC), and simultaneously 'incorporated' polytechnics as independent bodies, outside the local authority framework and with their own national funding council (the Polytechnics and Colleges Funding Council [PCFC]). The 1992 Act performed a similar service for FE colleges, but also crucially unified and then redistributed the Higher Education Funding Councils on a territorial basis (with separate Councils for England, Scotland and Wales), along with granting (by statute) degree-awarding powers to polytechnics and large colleges meeting certain criteria and the right of polytechnics to use the title 'university'. Prior to this dramatic shift there had been a mad rush by certain institutions to meet the numerical and other criteria for polytechnic and then university status, the consequences of which are still unfolding in both funding and reputational terms.

Clarke moved on swiftly after the 1992 Act and was succeeded by perhaps the least popular of the Conservative Secretaries of State across the sector. John Patten confessed to the Committee of Vice-Chancellors and Principals (CVCP) in 1993 that he had no vision for the future of higher education, and was also caught in possession of the policy football when the Treasury woke up to the fact that in allowing institutions to expand at marginal costs (on the basis of the local authority fee only), they had opened up an uncapped commitment to pay both fees and maintenance to the extra students. At the same time concerns about quality and standards came to the fore. The result was a cap on further full-time expansion, euphemistically termed 'consolidation', a sense of bad faith across the sector, and the mix of ingredients leading to the financial crisis that precipitated the Dearing Inquiry.

Taking stock of these changes it is hard to avoid the conclusion that collectively they represent a significant reduction in autonomy for the traditional universities and a significant gain in independence for the polytechnics and colleges. Before the 1988 and 1992 Acts the 'university' system was largely as bequeathed by Robbins, relatively generously resourced and managed with a light touch by the UGC. The 'public sector' was firmly under both local and central control. Academic standards and validation of courses were almost exclusively operated through the central charter of the Council for National Academic Awards (CNAA), and funding allocations (from the early 1980s) driven through the National Advisory Body for Public Sector Higher Education (the 'NAB') coordinating the allocation of places from the Advanced Further Education pool of the Department for Education and Science (DES) with an iron hand. It is no wonder that leaders of institutions from the two former sectors look back with such different feelings on their recent past.

From Baker to Dearing and Beyond

The next question is of course about the size, shape and key characteristics of a 'post-Dearing' system, especially in the light of the likely reactions of a new Labour government. As set out in the sample of submissions to Dearing in figure 1.10, almost everybody agrees that further growth is necessary, although with varying degrees and types of condition attached.

Diversity and Institutional Status

Figure 1.11 demonstrates what this period of expansion and reform has done to the pattern of higher education institutions since Robbins. Most commentators welcome the diversity that this has apparently brought to the system,

Figure 1.10   Calls for expansion post-Dearing

- **Confederation of British Industry 1994**
  'Thinking ahead; ensuring the expansion of higher education into the 21st century'

'The Government's approach should be fundamentally revised so that the UK aims for a minimum graduation target of 40 per cent — rather than a participation target of 33 per cent — of young people by the year 2000. This figure does not represent a final target — if the demand for higher education continues to increase in line with current trends, employers see no reason why a 45 per cent or even 50 per cent target among young people should not be envisaged.'

- **Council for Industry and Higher Education 1995**
  'A Wider Spectrum of Opportunities'

'The pool of young people qualified to apply to universities is planned to expand by 2000 from the present one-third to at least a half of the 18-year-old age group. Government and employers are already discussing whether to raise that 50 per cent target to a higher one of 66 per cent.'

- **Committee of Vice-Chancellors and Principals 1995**
  'The growth in student numbers in British higher education'

'The Government's target of a 33 per cent participation rate for under 21s by 2000 . . . now seems relatively modest by international standards. CVCP believes that a 40 per cent Age Participation Index for 18–19-year-olds by the year 2000/01 is a reasonable target.'

- **National Union of Students 1996**
  'Opportunity, diversity and partnership — the student agenda for higher education'

'NUS believes that there should be planned expansion in higher education provision over the next 20 years. NUS has argued that the target for the age participation rate should be at least 40 per cent of 18-year-olds to enter higher education in the medium term. We believe that a realistic target for 20 years' time would be 50 per cent of that age group.'

Figure 1.11   Number of universities, UK, 1950–95

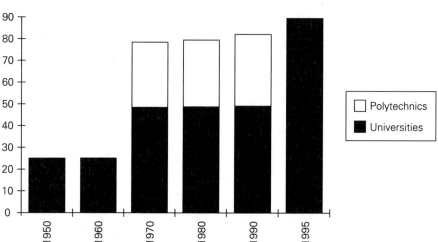

Source: CIHE, 1996b.

principally from the perspective of increased choice for students. There are, however, attendant worries about 'mission convergence' (a better term than the 'academic drift' associated with the new universities after Robbins) and the maintenance of both quality and standards (Watson, 1997, forthcoming).

Decoding Dearing on diversity is an essential element of any accurate reading of the Report. For Dearing on diversity the watchwords are differentiation and discipline, as discussed below in terms of the pattern of institutions providing higher education (chapters 10, 13 and 16) and quality and standards (chapter 11).

Just as the Committee could find no substantial body of opinion against further expansion (on the right terms), so 'diversity' was also uniformly presented in submissions as an unqualified good. Often such statements were allied to charges against government, against the funding councils, and against professional bodies for actions they have apparently taken to increase homogeneity and conformity of the system. The Committee partly upheld such charges, but also pointed to actions taken by institutions themselves to converge, or at least to spread (in order to reduce risk) their mission-based objectives (NCIHE, 1997, Main Report 3.90–92). The outcome is a strong endorsement of diversity within a framework, of understanding about institutional status and title, of agreement upon the pattern and standards of awards, and of explicit missions in such fields as research and regional development. For Dearing the notion of diversity as an excuse, or explanation of failure to live up to an accountable role within the national system is unacceptable, and is seen as not in higher education's best interests. Without it, autonomy (another uniformly endorsed 'good') will be in danger (ibid., Main Report 10.102).

Responding to Dearing

The key relevant recommendations from the Dearing Inquiry are as follows:

We recommend to the government that it should have a long-term strategic aim of responding to increased demand for higher education, much of which we expect to be at sub-degree level; and that to this end, the cap on full-time undergraduate places should be lifted over the next two to three years and the cap on full-time sub-degree places should be lifted immediately (recommendation 1).

We recommend to the government and the funding bodies that diversity of institutional mission, consistent with high quality delivery and the responsible exercise of institutional autonomy, should continue to be an important element of the United Kingdom's higher education system; and that this should be reflected in the funding arrangements for institutions (recommendation 61).

We recommend to the funding bodies and the research councils that they review their mainstream teaching and research funding arrangements to ensure they do not discourage collaboration between institutions; and that, where appropriate, they encourage collaboration. We recommend to the funding bodies that they be prepared to use their funds on a revolving basis, bringing forward and offsetting annual allocations in support of collaboration which has a strong educational and financial rationale (reommendation 68).

We recommend to the Quality Assurance Agency that, as it develops its arrangements, it ensures that these arrangements do not discourage collaboration between institutions (recommendation 69).

The main themes emerging from Dearing's evaluation of the problems and prospects of the system as a whole are thus:

1   the need to respond to demand, and thereby return to growth, coupled with;
2   an assumption that a key feature of the resulting increase in numbers will be both demand and support for sub-degree qualifications;
3   the channelling of provision through a clear pattern of institutions, differentiated by status, title and mission, and hence a 'disciplined diversity' of provision (see also chapter 16); and
4   measures to restore, and in many instances newly create, collaborative frameworks of provision, to succeed a period of officially encouraged competition.

Each of these predictions and injunctions implies a tough challenge to the system as it is currently configured and operates. The sector as a whole, as the analysis below is intended to make clear, may face difficulties in channelling demand into sub-degree courses, in sorting out the boundary between further and higher education, and in creating (or perhaps 'restoring') a sense of collaboration after a decade and a half of politically-hyped and organizationally enervating competition.

2 Changes in Society, the Economy and Politics

HE and National Competitiveness

Ever since the first significant expansion of UK higher education, beyond the golden triangle of Oxford, Cambridge and London, in the early nineteenth century, the sponsors and supporters of the enterprise have wanted to enlist it in the war against national, regional and local economic decline.

The most recent expression of this aim, and one of the most comprehensive, is the development and eventual endorsement of National Education and Training Targets (NETTs), but this initiative merely echoes in a more comprehensive fashion the aims of such government department programmes as 'Enterprise in Higher Education' (initially from the Manpower Services Commission and then the Department of Employment) and 'Technology Foresight' (of the newly-created Office of Science and Technology).

The overall aim described in the 1995 NETTs statement was:

> To improve the UK's international competitiveness by raising standards and attainment levels in education and training to world class levels through ensuring that:
>
> 1 All employers invest in employee development to achieve business success.
> 2 All individuals have access to education and training opportunities, leading to recognized qualifications, which meet their needs and aspirations.
> 3 All education and training develops self-reliance, flexibility and breadth, in particular through fostering competence in core skills.

Figure 2.1 summarizes the national targets eventually arrived at and the latest data on their achievement (August 1997). The penultimate objective, relating to NVQ 4 qualifications, has major implications for HE, as is discussed in Part 3 below. After an early spurt of achievement towards the target, the effects of 'consolidation' have slowed progress significantly, and this looks likely to be one of a number of the targets not reached by the millennium.

Dearing's scoping of the international horizon falls in neatly with such objectives, not least in terms of the report's emphasis on the threat of China and the 'Asian tigers'. But it also catches a more socially egalitarian and emancipatory tone, in terms of individual entitlement and social as well as economic returns on higher education investment.

Most importantly, however, the society for which Dearing is prescribing and designing an educational system (in this and his related reports on the

Figure 2.1   Progress towards national education and training targets in the UK

Target	Autumn 1996 Position	Target for December 2000
• **Foundation Target 1** 19-year-olds with five GCSEs at Grade C or above, an Intermediate GNVQ or an NVQ level 2	70.2%	85%
• **Foundation Target 2** 19-year-olds qualified to level 2 in communication, numeracy and IT[1]	9.7%	75%
21-year-olds qualified to level 3 in communication, numeracy and IT[2]	0.4%	35%
• **Foundation Target 3** 21-year-olds with two GCE A levels, an Advanced GNVQ or an NVQ level 3	46.4%	60%
• **Lifetime Target 1** Proportion of the workforce with NVQ level 3, Advanced GNVQ or two GCE A levels	41.8%	60%
• **Lifetime Target 2** Proportion of the workforce with NVQ level 4 or above	23.9%	30%
	March 1997 Position	
• **Lifetime Target 3** Organizations with 200 or more staff, recognized as Investors in People	20.9%	70%
Organizations with 50 or more staff, recognized as Investors in People	10.1%	35%

1 The figures are for GB. They relate only to those with GCSE grades A*–C in English, Maths and IT, SCE Standard Grade 1–3 or a full GNVQ at Advanced or Intermediate level. It has been agreed that some other qualifications can be included in the measurement of progress towards this target, but the sources of data for these additional qualifications are fairly new and they are not included here.
2 The figures are for GB, they relate only to those with a GNVQ at Advanced level.
Source: NACETT, 1997.

compulsory phase and 16–19) is dramatically different from that encountered by Robbins.

From Robbins to Dearing: Continuity and Change

There have been many changes in the socioeconomic context of higher education since the Robbins Report was published in 1963. However, the overall structure and dynamics of the wider society remain fundamentally unchanged since the 1960s. The economy is, if anything, more dominated in the 1990s than the 1960s by capitalist, free-market structures and ideology, both nationally and internationally. As Ralph Miliband (1994) has argued

> . . . capitalism is more firmly embedded in the social order than it ever was, notwithstanding all the transformations which it has undergone over the years. Market relations are insistently praised as the most desirable form of individual and social interaction; and there never has been a time when commercialization has more thoroughly come to pervade all spheres of life. (p. 10)

Economic, political and social changes in the 34 years between the two reports have nevertheless been profound. Economically, as is well-known, Britain has declined in relation to the nations with which it is traditionally compared. This has not been a characteristic peculiar to the last three decades; the British economy has been in steady, relative decline since at least the 1920s and arguably since the late nineteenth century. By 1991 we were eighteenth, in terms of living standards, amongst the 24 countries in membership of the Organization for Economic Cooperation and Development (OECD) and eighth among the 12 member states of the European Union (EU) (National Commission on Education, 1993, p. 15).

Successive governments in the 1960s and 1970s grappled with the interlinked problems of inflation, balance of payments deficits, low investment, declining competitiveness, and (after 1973) persistently increasing unemployment. The full-blooded neo-liberalism of the Thatcher era had its origins, both ideological and economic, in the Heath and Wilson/Callaghan governments of the 1970s and their attempts to cope with the aftermath of the oil crisis and subsequent depression of 1973 (see Coates, 1980). Thatcherism has undoubtedly left its legacy both economically and socially — and indeed politically, as is discussed below. Economically, the 'pure', extreme form of monetarism had a predictably short life but it did hasten already existing trends of deindustrialization, outflow of capital and consequent low investment, and rising unemployment. The persistent dominance of finance capital was also exacerbated considerably during the 1980s, (see Anderson, 1965) and concerted attacks were made on organized labour, for example the miners during the prolonged strike of 1984–85.

This predominantly negative economic record needs to be contextualized internationally, and qualified to an extent as a result of the changed political and ideological environment of the later 1990s. Internationally, the period since 1963 has certainly seen increasing economic globalization and interdependence. Multinational companies, with the resources and power to seek the most cost-effective locations for production irrespective of national boundaries, have become far more dominant. The increasing sophistication of technology has been a powerful aid to this process, in terms of telecommunications, transport, IT and many other features of economic life. The growing power of such enterprises, independent to a large extent of national governments, is a significant aspect of the economic environment, which continues to be characterized centrally by commitments to profit-making and competition, and by an ethos of individualism.

This overall economic configuration determines the labour market context within which higher education in the UK will operate. There is, and will be increasingly, a demand for a more flexible workforce, equipped to a high level with not only specific, relevant disciplinary knowledge but with generic, transferable skills. As the Kennedy Report on participation in further education makes clear, (Kennedy, 1997) there is an urgent economic need not only for continued expansion of higher education but for an increase in FE level provision. If the National Targets for Education and Training are to be achieved, there needs to be significant expansion of all post-compulsory provision, as well as more effective preparation during compulsory phases.

Many of the social trends in the UK since the 1960s reflect these economic changes. The decline of manufacturing and extractive industry, and the dominance of global capitalism, have been a prime cause of the weakening of trade unionism, and indeed of collectivist thought and organizational formations generally. There is little sign, in the late 1990s, of New Labour reversing this downgrading of trade union power and influence. Nevertheless, it is important to note the continuing objective importance of trade unions. Approximately eight million people in Britain are members of TUC affiliated trade unions, and the unions continue to occupy a key place in the Labour Party's structure.

Economic change has produced a very different environment for graduate employment. The increasing emphasis upon service, finance and professional sector occupations mean that generic skills — and specific 'new' skills, such as creativity, design, marketing and IT and organizational ability — have assumed a new importance (as discussed in chapter 8). There has also been a growth of employment in small and medium sized companies, and this can be seen as part cause and part effect of a growing trend of atomized, individualistic structures and attitudes in the workplace: post-industrial social formations and post-Fordist models of production, as post-modern analysis would have it (Usher et al., 1997, p. 2). With this development have come flatter management structures, an emphasis upon quality assurance and the need for a multiskilled and flexible workforce (ibid.).

Trends in family structure and the pattern of female employment have similarly economic and social dimensions. The traditional nuclear family, characterized by a permanent and early marriage, the bearing of children at an early age, and women remaining in the house rather than in paid employment, has become far less prevalent since the 1960s. People marry at an older age, more women remain childless, and those who do have children have fewer and start their families later in life (HMSO, 1996). There is an increasing number of single parent families.

Many more women work, mainly part-time; divorce rates are much higher; and there has, generally, been a marked increase in 'gender awareness' in society. In all these ways, women generally — but middle-class women in particular — have become far more independent since the 1960s, though economic and social inequality of gender is still prevalent. (These and related social factors are discussed in the context of 'lifelong learning and the common culture' in chapter 18.)

Partly as a result of the growth of telecommunications and IT, global culture has become another dominant characteristic of the 1990s. In part, this is simply the proliferation of gadgetry, with access to the predominantly American and largely conformist 'products' transmitted: television in all its increasingly commercialized forms, video, Internet, et al. This has been described as a process of 'global cultural convergence, the production of universal cultural products and global market consumers' (Kenway et al., 1997). It is also, however, an increasingly important means of socializing the population into homogeneous, international culture whose primary political consequence is to provide persistent and seductive legitimation of the existing social and economic order (see Miliband, 1969). Post-modern analysts, however, go on to emphasize both the importance of the local community and of consumers and consumption *per se* within the new cultural formations. Equally important, they claim, is the breaking down, within post-modernism, of the old elitist barriers between high culture and popular culture (Usher et al., 1997).

The essential point remains that these cultural changes, and most of the other social changes noted, have dual and paradoxical implications as far as higher education is concerned; they point both to an increased plurality, flexibility and heterogeneity, and to an increased social and cultural uniformity and common, and conformist, culture and common sense.

These changes in structure and attitude are mirrored in political change since the 1960s. The assault by Thatcherism on the post-war political orthodoxy, centred on the welfare state and the mixed economy, was dramatic but short-lived. Politically, the most important legacies of this atypical period may be seen as: first, the resurgence of the Conservative right-wing, anti-consensual nationalism, deeply opposed to the European Union; and secondly, the decisive shifting of the spectrum of British politics to the right, the principal consequence being the destruction of old Labour and the creation of the centrist New Labour Party and its triumphant rise to power in the 1997 General Election.

In terms of HE, the impact of this political change has been profound. The ideological shift has paved the way for the acceptance of a system financed in increasingly large part by non-public sources, principally the individual students and employers. It has also given further emphasis to the trends towards more vocationally oriented provision and employer partnerships.

However, both Thatcherism and, in a different sense, New Labour are also populist in orientation. This too underlies the support for the creation of a mass system of higher education. Central to this commitment, is a now contentious ideology of support for 'equality of opportunity'. To explain the debate surrounding issues of equality takes us to the heart of an important issue for higher education and, more widely, for the long-term policy orientation of the New Labour government.

There can be no doubt that Britain, already a deeply unequal society at every level, has become considerably more unequal over the 18 years of Conservative government from 1979. This was a result in large part of deliberate policy. Several measures introduced early in the Thatcher years give clear indication of this: for example, the specific policy to lower the higher tax rate to 40 per cent, and the general deflationary policy designed to reduce wage costs, labour power and, it was argued, inflation, by increasing unemployment. By 1993, '10 per cent of the population . . . owned 50 per cent of all wealth, and . . . 25 per cent owned 71 per cent. In other words, 75 per cent of the population had to make do with 29 per cent of the remaining wealth' (Miliband, 1994, p. 17). Similarly, approximately one-third of families now live below the poverty line as calculated, for example, by NCH-Action for Children (NCH-Action for Children, 1996). The life chances of both young people and of adults seeking employment (and education and training) from such backgrounds are demonstrably unsatisfactory.

There is no disagreement within New Labour that such a situation needs redress, but deep disagreement about how best to achieve such reform. The interchange between Roy Hattersley and Gordon Brown in articles in the *Guardian* in August 1997 illustrates the divisions. Hattersley argues that the core commitment of social democracy has to be to equality of opportunity and, to achieve this, to redistribution of wealth and opportunity (Hattersley, 1997). Brown sees this as old Labour ideology and argues instead for the lateral thinking of his 'welfare to work' proposals whereby the cycle of disadvantage will be broken by innovative education and training opportunities for the disadvantaged, particularly the young unemployed (Brown, 1997).

Whatever the solutions, there can be no disputing the problem. If the New Labour Party political project is to have significant, lasting impact the inequalities of contemporary society have to be at least reduced. There are not only inequalities of wealth and income, important though these are, but inequalities of power — at work, in the community, and in political, social and economic life generally.

It is hardly surprising that higher education, in terms both of the social class make-up of its student body and of its culture and ethos, reflects these inequalities. Overwhelmingly, the beneficiaries of the expansion of higher education since the 1960s have been the middle classes, broadly defined. (For further discussion of this, see chapter 4.) To the extent that participation has been widened in the 1990s, this has been very largely within a relatively few, and predominantly new universities.

Responding to Dearing

The challenge to universities in this context is thus to widen participation through a variety of possible mechanisms — access oriented admissions policies, curriculum development and so on. However, equally important is the challenge to adapt and develop the universities' definition of their fundamental purposes. Does the creation of a mass system of higher education, with the widened participation advocated by the Dearing Report, require such a reevaluation? Specifically, in the context of the discussion over inequality, should universities have a 'social purpose', over and above their straightforwardly economic roles, to develop a lifelong learning culture that embodies egalitarian social perspectives? And where does the commitment to the liberal philosophy of education fit into this new structure? These are issues returned to in Parts 5 and 6 below.

3   Europe and Lifelong Learning

The Dearing Committee conducted its business with a keen awareness of the characteristics of higher education in partner countries in the European Union. Visits were made to France, Germany and the Netherlands, as a result of which comparative views of qualifications, standards and the student experience were derived. A report was also commissioned from the Higher Education Quality Council (HEQC), and published by the Committee, on higher education frameworks elsewhere in Europe (NCIHE, 1997, Appendix 5).

One central conclusion was that the UK probably leads the way in continuing education (CE) and particularly continuing vocational education (CVE) provision. In this context it is useful to reflect on the sources and record of the European Union's most sustained foray into the field of lifelong learning.

The European Year of Lifelong Learning

The original impetus for the European Year of Lifelong Learning (EYLL) came from a European Union paper in 1993 entitled *Growth, Competitiveness, Employment*. The European Union, and, increasingly, the governments of the constituent nation states, recognized that 'lifelong learning' for the mass of the population was a formative element in the international economy. The EU paper set out two alternative futures:

> one where a small number of people enjoyed secure and stimulating work, and many looked forward to casual short-term low paid work alternating with unemployment. The other described a world in which we invest in the skills of all the people, in the confident belief that wherever there is surplus skill and talent new economies arise to make use of it. (Tuckett, 1997, p. 6)

The background to the argument is familiar: the rapidly changing technology and economic structure of Western societies; the consequent need for a more highly trained and flexible workforce; and the demographic projections of an ageing workforce and society into the twenty-first century. These and related influences constitute a strong case for a radical revision and extension of post-compulsory education which should be characterized by a recognition that education *throughout and beyond* 'working life' is essential. It is also inherent in such social analyses, however, that there is an equal need for learning to underpin economic prosperity and learning to foster and develop a democratic, informed and participative society. While the former can be justified in straightforwardly vocational, pragmatic terms, the latter is dependent upon a series of more philosophical assertions and arguments (see Taylor et al., 1985).

There is a continuing tension between these two elements of lifelong learning, and, as Alan Tuckett has pointed out, these were evident in the EYLL — as they were in more extreme form in the post-compulsory education contexts of many individual EU nation states, including the UK (Tuckett, 1997). Quite clearly, however, the vocational and economic imperatives dominated EU thinking in this area, as is indicated in the very title of the 1993 EU paper cited above.

The European programmes LEONARDO and SOCRATES, although in theory they cover the full spectrum of lifelong learning development, have in practice reinforced the EU's concentration upon vocational training initiatives.

The EYLL, as indeed the concept and practice of lifelong learning itself, spans the whole of post-compulsory education and training and the majority of EYLL activity in the UK as elsewhere was in the 'non-HE' sectors. The emphases were replicated throughout all post-compulsory sectors. In the UK, the policy for the EYLL followed on from the marked increase in adult participation in education and training following the 1992 Further and Higher Education Act. This has been described as 'perhaps the biggest fillip to adult participation in vocational and academic education' (ibid., p. 8). By the mid-1990s, three in four students in FE were aged over 21, and, in HE, as noted above (chapter 1), there has also been a rapid increase in adult participation. The UK government's National Education and Training Targets, as revised in 1995, indicate clearly the objectives of policy in this area (see chapter 2). Finally, it is important to note that this broad perspective was shared across the major political parties up to the 1997 General Election.

The UK's priorities for the EYLL reflected these concerns, which fitted broadly with the objectives identified by the European Council of Ministers and the European Parliament. It was agreed that the UK's priorities within the year's key themes should be:

- adults in work, to emphasize individuals' responsibility for lifelong learning, and the important role of employers including smaller firms;

- higher education, including promotion of part-time study, links with businesses, non-traditional routes and transfer of technology especially to SMEs;

- information, advice and guidance on continuing education and training for adults and careers guidance;

- adult education, including opportunities for older workers; and

- young people preparing for work (14–19-year-olds), including promotion of initial vocational training and business-linked projects (DfEE, 1995).

Figure 3.1 EYLL themes (1996)

• the importance of a high quality general education, open to all without discrimination, as a preparation for lifelong learning;

• promoting vocational training leading to qualifications as a basis for:
   * a smooth transition to working life
   * further personal development
   * adapting to a changing job market
   * equality of opportunities between men and women;

• promoting continuing education and training, especially in relation to new requirements in the world of work;
• motivating individuals, especially from under-represented groups, toward lifelong learning;
• promoting links between education and training providers and business, particularly involving small and medium sized companies;
• promoting to both sides of industry the importance of lifelong learning in the contexts of European competitiveness and economic growth;
• promoting to parents the importance to their children of education and lifelong learning;
• development of the European dimension of initial and continuing education and training.

Source: DfEE, 1995.

Figure 3.1 sets out the Commission's eight themes for the work of the year.

In addition to centrally promoted European activities, each member state was allocated relatively modest funding for nationally based project development. In the UK, £400,000 was made available and the UK government, using National Institute of Adult and Continuing Education (NIACE) as the administering agency, gave priority to five themes: adults in work; HE; information, advice and guidance; adult education; young people preparing for work. There were several sub-areas identified which were of particular concern for HE: lifelong learning in small and medium sized enterprises (SMEs) (though links with FE were the primary focus here); part-time study in HE; the development of business/higher education institution (HEI) links and of non-traditional routes into HE; and the transfer of technology, especially to SMEs.

A large number of innovative projects were funded in the UK through the EYLL programme. (The full listing was published by the Department for Education and Employment [DfEE] in 1997.) These spanned FE, HE and the voluntary sector and included not only community-based provision for individuals and groups not previously involved with education but also a wide variety of partnership developments — with employees, with television companies, with the TUC, with IT specialist companies, and so on.

While it is difficult to quantify or evaluate the results of such initiatives, it is clear that significant numbers of adult students benefited. Undoubtedly the high profile of Adult Learners Week, coordinated by NIACE, made a real impact:

10,000 people phoned the 'Helpline' (and 40 per cent of them subsequently enrolled on courses); a Parliamentary reception attended by the education spokespersons of all the major parties was organized; 5,000 local events took place with extensive media coverage. As Alan Tuckett concludes in his NIACE survey of the EYLL, 'there is no doubt that the European Year has been successful in highlighting the case for Lifelong Learning in the UK' (Tuckett, 1997, p. 24).

Responding to Dearing

However, despite all the very real achievements of the EYLL both in the UK and elsewhere, there has been little coherent policy implementation in the post-compulsory sector to facilitate lifelong learning either in the EU or in individual nation states. This applies particularly in HE where, in most EU countries, universities have shown little commitment to lifelong learning — and governments have shown correspondingly little enthusiasm for such a policy initiative.

As this short survey reveals there is much unfinished business for continuing higher education across the European Union. The UK's lead in both the provision of part-time general higher education and policy for and delivery of continuous professional development may be short-lived, and not entirely relevant. After all, an increasing number of UK graduates in professional fields are going to want their qualifications to have currency across the EU (as, for example, they do already in nursing and midwifery). Equally, the growing sense of dislocation between exit standards of degrees and diplomas awarded in the UK and elsewhere in the Union, however poorly grounded in evidence, requires systematic attention.

Part 2

Participation

4   Getting into Higher Education

As indicated above (chapter 1) greater fairness in the distribution of the benefits of higher education (by age, gender, class, and disability) has critically been a concomitant of growth, but by no means a linear one. Growth has meant increased fairness, but this has been a painfully slow process and in some cases the gap has been widening.

Participation and Fairness

As the Dearing Report definitively exposes, the key problem is social class, and the uneven social equity performance of expansion. Probably the most arresting chart in the main report is 7.1 (reproduced below as figure 4.1) which shows the dramatically disproportionate take-up of places from the top two socioeconomic groups.

Time-series analyses (including one going back to 1991 submitted by the DfEE in their evidence to Dearing [see chapter 1, figure 1.6]) expose this anomaly even more cruelly.

Earlier data is patchy, and it is hard to establish a secure time line. But the study by Smithers and Robinson for the Council for Industry and Higher Education (CIHE) drawn on for figure 4.2 (below) shows both the disproportionate role of the ex-PCFC sector in any improvement of the figures, and the response of the 'traditional system' when, as in the early 1980s, numbers were squeezed. It appears that when admissions tutors can act conservatively on this dimension they will.

When allied to the data in chapter 12 about the regressive nature of the maintenance system in HE this evidence forces us to the conclusion that, however slow and non-linear its effect, further expansion is necessary for fairness.

Information and Advice

Associated with the market ideology of Conservative thinking on higher education was the primacy of student choice. However, as in many other contexts, this supposed commitment to populist democracy conflicted with the government's

Figure 4.1   Percentage of home full-time degree programme entrants, 1994

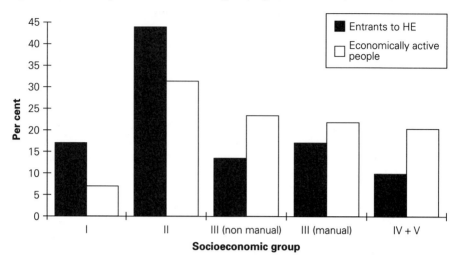

Source: NCIHE, 1997, Chart 7.1.

Figure 4.2   Participation by social classes III–V, 1979–93

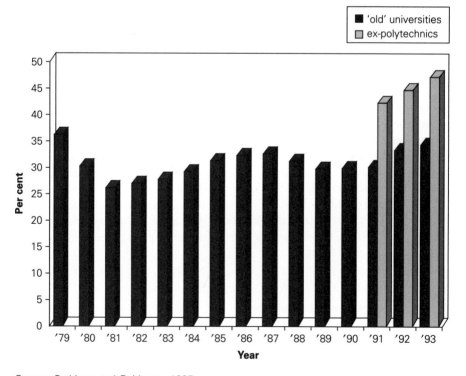

Source: Smithers and Robinson, 1995.

ideological agenda. As it emerged that student choice and governmental preference for choice of study were imperfectly aligned (as in the preference of
the majority for arts and humanities over applied science and technology), a
new term of art was coined: 'informed choice'. A problem is that, instrumental
though students may be when choosing options in post-compulsory education
(see chapter 10 below), their choices will rarely match central assumptions in
human resources planning.

Part of the problem lies in the uneasy relationship between marketing and
advice and guidance in the role of both further and higher education institutions.
In the latter case, part of the remit of the HEQC is to keep an eye on the accuracy
and probity of institutions' promotional material. Informal pressure may have
resulted in some cases, but there is very little reflection of this work in the
Council's published reports on domestic provision; concerns have been more
readily expressed about overseas provision (HEQC, 1996a).

As the battle between sixth-form colleges and FE providers has been intensified, with funding crucially at stake, there is evidence of institutional need outweighing the best interest of students at the post-16 level in particular. So far
there is little echo of such problems at the HE level (with the possible exception of traditional universities 'poaching' students in Clearing offered places on
HNDs in science and engineering by the new universities), but it remains a
cautionary tale.

Dearing's solution, echoing directly the UACE submission, is to ensure
wherever possible independent sources of advice and guidance to students
and potential students at critical points in their learning careers.

Beyond UCAS

Lifelong learning not only implies a system of exit from higher education with
banked credit and intermediate qualifications (see chapter 7), but also a system of entry that is no longer dominated by the special needs of 18 or 19-year-
old school leavers. Not only does a majority of new entrants to all forms of
higher education now apply for entry to higher education with their prior qualifications securely in hand, but the system of 'provisional' or 'conditional' entry
to higher education run through the Universities and Colleges Admissions Service
(UCAS) largely for final year sixth-formers and other 'A' level candidates has
begun to creak. The problems relate not only to volume of work and timing
(especially the gap between results confirmation by the 'A' level examination
boards and finalization of university entrance), but also to the decreasing relevance and equity of the so-called 'insurance' system of held second offers. An
increasing number of candidates just missing their first offer are opting out of
the system for a year or more rather than being held to another offer whose
requirements they have easily exceeded.

Putting all of these pressures together — the increased number of 'non-
standard entrants', especially those already holding their qualifications, and

growing concerns about the second-chance or Clearing system and the necessary rigidity of the rules which govern it — the logic of a post-qualification system (PQA) seems inescapable. Several models and options have been devised and touted (not least by a CVCP working party [CVCP, 1997b]) but they all expose the difficulties of getting from here to there. In particular the group of traditional universities whose places are very largely filled by the second choices of the 'Oxbridge' fall-out is profoundly hostile. Another problem is the potential squeeze on the time specialist courses need for interviewing (as in teacher education) or viewing of examples of work (as in art and design, and for a range of GNVQ candidates).

Dearing also sees the future in terms of a PQA system, but has no specific prescription on who should take responsibility for carrying the development forward, or how.

Modernizing Matriculation

The conservative tendency of admissions tutors has been alluded to above in terms of the origins of students. Another growing source of tension concerns perceptions of the intellectual, and especially the disciplinary preparation of students. There is a growing chorus of university teachers, notably in the sciences and engineering, bemoaning the lack of preparation of their new first year students for the higher education experience they have traditionally supplied. A small part of this can be put down to misplaced nostalgia — as Sir Ron Dearing noted in a witty section of his 16–19 report, educational standards were always much higher 20 years ago, even when they palpably were not (Dearing, 1996, p. 6 and pp. 46–7). More serious problems probably arise from the variety and breadth of pre-matriculation courses and some occasionally ill-founded notions of equivalence. The universities' problems at this level are also exposing severe difficulties within schools, especially in science, technology and languages. The National Commission on Education, among others, has pointed to the vicious circle of poor teaching in key areas, leading to lack of preparation for higher education and then further problems of teacher supply (NCE, 1993, p. 198).

One response has been to design longer courses, especially in professional and technical areas, although this has come up against (not always consistent) resistance from the funding councils and the DfEE. European equivalences are often appealed to here. Another has been to make careful use of modular programmes, especially in the earlier stages to design and deliver 'balancing' components, to improve the prospects of students with more or less equal levels of competence tackling higher level components. Dearing's approach (see the recommendations below) is to encourage a greater concentration on the skills rather than the knowledge components in prior qualifications.

Responding to Dearing

The key relevant recommendations from the Dearing Inquiry are as follows:

We recommend to the government and the funding bodies that, when allocating funds for the expansion of higher education, they give priority to those institutions which can demonstrate a commitment to widening participation, and have in place a participation strategy, a mechanism for monitoring progress, and provision for review by the governing body of achievement (recommendation 2).

We recommend that, with immediate effect, the bodies responsible for funding further and higher education in each part of the UK collaborate and fund — possibly jointly — projects designed to address low expectations and achievement and to promote progression to higher education (recommendation 3).

We recommend that the funding bodies consider financing, over the next two to three years, pilot projects which allocate additional funds to institutions which enrol students from particularly disadvantaged localities (recommendation 4).

We recommend that, over the medium term, the representative bodies, in consultation with other relevant agencies, should seek to establish a post-qualification admissions system (recommendation 10).

We recommend that:

- *institutions of higher education, over the medium term, integrate their careers services more fully into academic affairs and that the provision of careers education and guidance is reviewed periodically by the Quality Assurance Agency;*

- *the government, in the medium to long term, should integrate careers advice for lifelong learning, to complement services based inside higher education institutions (recommendation 11).*

We recommend to institutions of higher education that, over the medium term, their admission procedures should develop to value good levels of competence in communication, numeracy and the practical use of information technology (recommendation 17).

We recommend to the government that, with immediate effect, it brings together the representative bodies of students, schools, colleges, higher education institutions and the organizations offering careers services to identify what better information is needed by students about higher education opportunities, their costs and benefits; and to work together to improve timely dissemination of the information (recommendation 85).

These recommendations imply significant urgency in the Committee's mind about the importance of the access and widening participation agenda, along with the endorsement of special initiatives (if not positive discrimination). They also assume a freeing up of the routes into higher education, with better-coordinated sources of advice to potential participants (which should, as far as possible, be independent of institutional special pleading), and a clearer, competence or skills-based understanding of the threshold to be achieved at the point of entry.

All of these elements should be welcomed in principle by the university, but key questions remain about how they are to be resourced. For example: who will staff or manage public careers service extended into higher education; will funding rewards for progress on widening participation be prospective (project-based) or retrospective? Equally there are significant problems of measurement and bench-marking to be resolved, as well as the automatic distrust by already hard-pressed institutions (especially those which are not successful in the competition) of top-slicing of overall grant and bidding for special initiatives.

5   Getting on in Higher Education

After Robbins, Kingsley Amis claimed that 'more' would mean 'worse' in higher education (Amis, 1960). After Baker, Sir Christopher Ball declared that 'more means different' (Ball, 1990). As our preceding analysis suggests, neither got it right. There is no evidence that substantially increased participation has meant a drop in student academic performance, or that Robbins' famous pool of people 'with the ability to benefit' has been used up; what evidence there is (from quality assessment and from degree results) suggests the opposite. Equally, the increased flexibility and responsiveness of the system, ideally creating a 'customer-friendly' pattern of participation (by mode of study, method of study, and level) anticipated by Sir Christopher has yet really to emerge (see chapter 7 on modularity). In this chapter we tackle three dimensions of this debate: the worry about falling standards; the concern to maintain and enhance 'efficiency'; and the real-world as opposed to the claimed flexibility and responsiveness of the system to both student needs and demands.

The Standards Debate

At every level of education in the UK, for the past decade or more, increased volume of entry to examinations seems to be accompanied by rising levels of achievement. Simultaneously, international 'spot-checks' on comparative attainment in such subjects as mathematics, science and languages appear to expose a system which is falling behind (Burghes, 1996). Higher education has not been immune to this form of analysis or paradoxical outcome. During the period of the post-Baker expansion we now know that the modal honours degree classification shifted upwards, from a lower to an upper second, and that this happened at a time when groups like admissions and first-year tutors (see chapter 4) and professional bodies (see chapter 10) became increasingly critical of educational outcomes (HEQC, 1996b).

For many commentators of the Kingsley Amis persuasion the notion of more people doing better just does not stand up. Mass participation will defeat the fundamental purposes of higher education. Their line of argument contains its own paradox: you can only prove standards are being maintained by showing that more people are doing worse. Across this minefield there are, however, one or two narrow but safer pathways. The difficult fact that the pessimists have to live with is that nearly all of the evidence on their side is anecdotal or judgmental in a flawed, usually autobiographical way. Education at all levels has changed, and has responded to a more complex and in many senses richer

Figure 5.1   British university entrants: 'A' level scores of home candidates accepted through UCCA, 1971–1991 (% with various scores)

Scores	3–8	9–12	13–15	
1971	28.0	46.7	25.3	
1976	29.8	43.9	26.2	
1981	24.2	45.7	30.0	
1984	14.8	49.3	35.7	
1988	16.6	48.5	34.9	(61,225)
Scores	**6–15**	**16–25**	**26–30**	
1989	12.6	54.2	33.2	(70,219)
1990	17.1	51.4	31.6	(80,251)
1991	17.7	51.0	31.2	(84,661)

Note: Only candidates with three or more 'A' levels are included and the best three counted with grade A = 5, B = 4, etc. before 1989. The scoring system was changed in 1989 to include AS qualifications.
Source: Halsey, 1993.

environment, itself a product of an increasingly pluralist society. This is reflected in the diversity of student experience, of young as well as of mature entrants. What is more, it continues to be the case throughout higher education, as the map of knowledge and the range of 'conversations' that students and staff engage in become more complex and diverse (see chapter 8).

Among the signposts to safer conclusions are analyses of entrants to higher education and the assessment of quality of the experience and achievements of students while they are on their courses. These can be supplemented by some coherent hypotheses about why student exit performance (the results accompanying their qualifications) continues to rise.

We have already examined above (chapter 4) the variety of matriculation qualifications and equivalent experience presented by new entrants. Figure 5.1 above is based upon work by A.H. Halsey for the National Commission on Education. It demonstrates how, even when you take the conservative assumption that the quality of the system is governed by the performance of students on the 'gold standard' of 'A' levels (to which successive governments have clung with such force) the case cannot be sustained that for those applicants for which this is the criterion, standards have fallen.

Performance while in higher education is benchmarked by systematic peer review. External examiners oversee the work of internal markers and the Boards of Examiners to which they are responsible in terms of the results assigned to individuals. Quality assessors and other 'visitors' from the relevant

academic and professional communities pass judgment on the overall performance of courses and programmes. Both forms of check and validation have
come in for criticism in recent years (as outlined in chapter 11), but importantly each has continued to work in a comprehensive, system-wide way. The
hard evidence from their work suggests, contrary to the anecdotal, finger-in-
the-wind approach of the system's critics that the UK framework of institutions
has indeed managed to maintain standards, at least up to the point where it
now faces the resourcing crisis set out below (chapter 13).

The external examining system has underwritten the pattern of steady
improvement in degree results. These in turn may be, as acknowledged by
Dearing, the product of changed modes of assessment (especially larger pro-
portions of coursework and projects, which have been shown to carry learning
benefits) (NCIHE, 1997, Main Report 9.40). Dearing also questions, as has a
growing number of commentators, the continued validity of the honours classification system itself, preferring that the real focus of collective quality assurance
should be on the 'threshold' for awards (ibid., Main Report 9.44).

Simultaneously, the results of quality assessment give more grounds for
reassurance than for concern. Figure 5.2 below summarizes the outcomes from
the two overview reports presented by the Higher Education Funding Council
for England's (HEFCE) Quality Assessment Committee: the first when the process was structured around a simple three-point scale ('excellent', 'satisfactory'
and 'unsatisfactory') and the second based upon a more complex 'graded
profile' where six aspects of provision are assessed on a four-point scale (grade
1 springs a verdict of 'not approved'). Similar results (especially the less than
1 per cent graded as 'unsatisfactory' or 'not approved') have been achieved in
Scotland and Wales. It may be argued that this process tests performance against
objectives set, institution by institution, and thus 'fitness for purpose' rather than
'fitness of purpose', but here again the discipline of collective assurance plays its
part. There is no secure evidence of any institution cynically 'aiming low' in
terms of the objectives it sets for its students, simply to pass the assessment test,

Figure 5.2   Outcomes of HEFCE's quality assessment 1992–95 and 1995–96

1992–1995	1995–1996
• 972 assessments • 553 assessment visits • 15 subject overview reports • 950 assessors	• 272 assessment visits • 8 subject overview reports • 440 assessors
Overall Outcomes:	**Overall Outcomes:**
• 26% Excellent • 73% Satisfactory • 1% Unsatisfactory	• 42.1% of all grades were 4 • 50.3% of all grades were 3 • 7.5% of all grades were 2 • 0.1% of all grades were 1

Source: HEFCE, 1995 and 1997.

or indeed of institutions successfully cheating the system through, for example, elaborate prior rehearsal.

The Royal Society, in a review of quality developments in research, concluded that external peer review has a number of problems: it tends to be retrospective and conservative; it is (unless carefully administered) prone to 'rings' and other forms of collusion; and does not necessarily carry confidence outside of the academic community. It is, however, the 'least worst' system available to us and hence worthy of continued support (Royal Society, 1995). It is thus important that on this measure (the only one securely available to us) the academic community itself has declared that quality has been maintained and standards are not falling.

Efficiency and Effectiveness

Another element of the pessimistic scenario of the effects of expansion is the prediction of declining effectiveness of the system as course lengths follow their European counterparts and are extended through student choice or necessity (for example, as greater numbers of formally full-time students hold down paying jobs) and as drop-out rates increase. By international comparison the UK system is remarkably efficient. Figure 5.3 shows the overall graduation rate of UK HE against OECD comparators. This is, of course, an important corrective

Figure 5.3   OECD: First degree (or equivalent) graduation rates, 1992

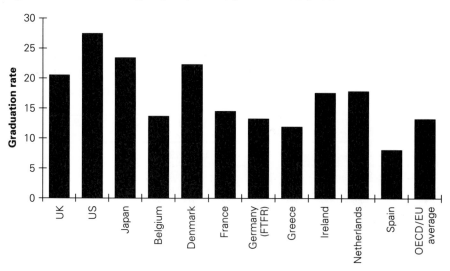

Note: Graduation rate — defined as the number of people graduating with Bachelors degrees, or Masters in some countries where it is the first degree obtained (Belgium, France and Germany), as a proportion of the population corresponding to the typical graduation age.
Source: IES, 1996.

to some of the data on our lower participation rates; the UK has been among the leaders in the business of turning students into graduates.

'Drop-out' is a subject hardly studied in the UK until very recently, and then largely because of the hints that funding councils might move towards a 'payment by results' regime. Indeed, only very recently has student data begun to be collected by the Higher Education Statistics Agency (HESA) in such a way that we can begin to track individuals' progress through the HE system. Such studies as there are (including by the DfEE) suggest, on the basis of crude cohort analyses, that a drop-out rate in the range of 14–18 per cent of each full-time cohort has worsened marginally if at all during the years of rapid expansion (NCIHE, 1997, Main Report, p. 395). There is no equivalent information on the progress of part-timers although formal non-completion is certain to be significantly higher. Measurement here is complex, not least because very large numbers of part-time adult students are studying in discrete modules or courses rather than award-bearing programmes.

Flexible Response?

The overall conclusion on the 'fit' between the evidence about progress through higher education and the lifelong learning agenda has to be that the major performance changes have still to happen. For example, the Robertson Report, *Choosing to Change*, found little evidence of widespread credit transfer activity, as opposed to its formal availability (Robertson, 1994). Our personal hypothesis is that arrangements for funding (of students and institutions) is a principal determinant of this under-performance (see chapter 12 and 13), but that institutions themselves also need to undergo some critical self-reflection before flexibility and responsiveness will be identified as rational and necessary priorities. Even then there are significant aspects of internal resistance to be overcome (HEQC, 1996c).

Responding to Dearing

Dearing's key relevant recommendation (in addition to all of those covered in our 'curriculum' chapters — for example on the framework of qualifications), centres on an authoritative national home for the framework of credit and a personal lifetime academic record.

We recommend that further work is done over the medium term, by the further and higher education funding bodies, the Higher Education Statistics Agency, and relevant government departments to address the creation of a framework for data about lifelong learning, using a unique student record number (recommendation 7).

There are some powerful potential inhibitors to institutions' willingness and ability to play together in terms of the qualifications framework, mutual recognition of credit, and ease of transfer and admission with advanced standing. Some are to do with internal (departmental) politics — those with an ample supply of students from 'traditional' routes are less likely to want to deal with 'special cases'. Even where there has been ample evidence of non-standard admission, the students concerned are often likely to be treated as the product of a kind of 'header tank' held in reserve until needed. Some are reputational — as in the cases where a university will declare the quality of its student output on the basis of the qualifications with which they were originally admitted (the progress of 'added value' as a mode of analysis in HE has been extremely slow). In making progress on these recommendations the Dearing 'carrots and sticks' identified in our discussions of quality and funding are probably of the greatest relevance. However, the Committee fails to address directly the issue of how to ensure that universities will have confidence in and use a credit framework. In the end, the mechanisms and formulae of the funding councils must be used, in our view, to reward those institutions which do develop in this area (and thereby, at least indirectly, penalize those which do not).

6   Coming Back to Higher Education

The traditional, elite university system was characterized by its homogeneity. Not only were the numbers of students and subsequent graduates a very small proportion of the population, they were drawn from a remarkably narrow socioeconomic range in terms of age, social class background, ethnicity and, until the post-Robbins era, gender (see chapter 1).

Adult 'Returners'

Most of these changes in the student population have taken place in the new universities and of course the Open University. However, it is important to note that rapid expansion of student numbers has also taken place, unevenly, in the traditional universities. Broadly, as discussed in chapter 2, this has been 'more of the same' in terms of student backgrounds and age profiles. Leslie Wagner has argued both that it is not surprising that 'the establishment of different institutions structurally distinct to carry out different functions legitimizes the traditional role of the traditional institutions'; and that the higher education system 'has become mass in its size but . . . remains elite in its values' (Wagner, 1995, pp. 19–20).

The context for 'returners' to higher education is thus highly complex. In the traditional, elite system, adult learners were largely provided for through university extra-mural departments — in one sense, a deficit or compensatory model of education open to the large bulk of adults who had not had the opportunity for mainstream higher education experience. But, for a substantial minority of extra-mural students, their adult studies led to entry onto degree schemes in the mainstream university, or to a place in one of the residential adult colleges, or to higher education level training. In many universities there were schemes, provided through extra-mural or Continuing Education departments, which catered specifically for different categories of 'returners': 'New Opportunities for Women' (NOW) programmes; certificated Access courses; and a range of 'mature matriculation' certificated schemes.

These were always the exception rather than the rule, however. The large bulk of adult students in CE programmes studied on a non-credit, non-award basis, and neither sought nor were offered access to mainstream awards. By the 1970s some universities — Kent, Hull and Manchester amongst them — did have part-time degree programmes organized and taught either by the CE department itself or, more often, by the department in conjunction with relevant subject departments in the university; but these again were on a small scale.

The mainstreaming and accreditation in England of over 90 per cent of previously non-credit bearing CE in 1995 required by the funding councils marked a fundamental change in CE provision in the traditional university sector. (Wales and Scotland have slightly different systems with Scotland in particular having significant variations in accreditation procedures.) While there were undoubtedly severe disadvantages with this process, both practical and ideological, mainstreaming was both inevitable and of potential long-term benefit for adult learners. The transition is proving difficult, and there has been evidence of student resistance: to assessment (although often tutors have more misgivings about this than the students); to the perceived bureaucracy; to the lack of flexibility; and not least to the increased level of student fees.

However, the long-term benefit of adult learners at last having their study on an explicitly equal footing with the mainstream student body is of over-riding importance. The opportunity now exists for universities to construct certificate, diploma, first degree and masters level programmes specifically for CE adult students, and based upon CE courses and modules. Potentially, there-fore, mainstreaming represents a most important access innovation. Whether this will really bring CE into the mainstream of the traditional university sys-tem, and thereby significantly change the culture and pedagogic practice of that system, remains to be seen. Evidence so far is that practice is likely to vary widely institution by institution. In some cases CE provision seems likely to become integrated with provision by other departments through a variety of 'internal CATS' arrangements. In other institutions CE provision has remained a largely separate activity and the accreditation given to CE courses has been 'self-contained' and perhaps thus of dubious value.

Overall, therefore, the traditional university sector now offers far greater opportunities for 'adult returners' than in the past. Most CE students continue to be registered for discrete credit for one or two courses or modules, rather than for awards *per se*. Statistical comparisons are therefore misleading. How-ever, potentially all CE students now registered in the traditional universities' CE programmes in England are part of the award-bearing structures of the higher education system.

By far the largest contribution to adult learners' access to higher education in the period since the 1980s has been in the other major sections of the system: the new universities and, separately and pre-eminently, the Open University.

The broad missions of the polytechnics, subsequently new universities, and of the Open University, were quite clear from the outset. The polytechnics were oriented 'to professional and vocational higher education more closely integrated with the world of employment', and the Open University to 'adults seeking a second or, in some cases, a first opportunity' (Wagner, 1995, p. 19). This has meant that a special focus on non-traditional, adult and continuing education has proved largely unnecessary in these more locally-oriented insti-tutions. For them continuing education has always been in the mainstream.

NIACE, in their Policy Discussion Paper *An Adult Higher Education,* (NIACE, 1993) emphasize that the large bulk of the expansion in student numbers has come from mature students (aged over 21 on entry), many of whom are studying part-time. '[G]rowth was three times as rapid for mature students generally as for young people, and most rapid among mature women' (ibid., p. 20). The paper usefully identifies four broad overlapping groups within this adult learner cohort: 'deferred beginners', usually in their twenties and studying full-time with standard student support from public sources (these represent approximately one-quarter of all mature entrants); 'returners', those who have experienced a change in domestic or work responsibility and seek HE opportunities as part of a reorientation (these are usually women in their thirties or early forties studying full-time and funded from public sources); 'developers', those seeking a qualitative improvement in skills and career prospects through HE (usually in the age range 30 to 50, strongly vocationally oriented, and usually funded through private sources or from employers); and 'enrichers', a wide range of adult learners of all ages but predominantly middle-aged who are seeking HE, normally part-time, for non-vocational, personal development reasons. Overall, mature student numbers in higher education more than doubled in the 1980s on both undergraduate and postgraduate degree programmes, and in both part-time and full-time modes.

These various categories of 'returners' have been a very large element in the constituencies and cultures of the new universities. Very many of them are also locally or regionally based, a characteristic they share with many of the standard age but non-standard background students. In general the new universities are pluralistic, multifaceted institutions with less of a monolithic culture. Nevertheless, the concept of lifelong learning is a dominant force and becoming more so, touching also some parts of the traditional university sector. At their best, the resulting programmes encompass a flexible approach to learning procedures, curriculum and pedagogic method and credit structures; and emphasize access and a symbiosis with the world of work.

Personal Testimony

This discussion has been at a level of some generality. To give examples of specific, real experiences this section concludes with case studies of HE experiences from adult learners in very different contexts. We have used, wherever appropriate, the students' own words.

Keith H. was born in 1950, the youngest of six and left school in 1965. After a short time spent at art school and a sampling of various jobs he followed his father and brothers into the mining industry. He stayed in the pits until after the 1984 miners' strike. The strike seemed to change everything for everyone in Yorkshire but for him things changed dramatically.

While in the pits he took an NUM sponsored day release course in industrial relations in the Department of Adult and Continuing Education of the University of Leeds. The Department sits in a peculiar position, on the edge of the main campus. For Keith and many others taking similar courses in that department, at that particular time, it represented a 'go-between', bridging two very different worlds: the world of mining, or colliery life, and the world of university life. Keith recalls that, 'the university had amazing reading facilities. Everyone on the miners' course took advantage of these facilities, especially in the departmental library. No one restricted their reading to industrial relations and labour issues.'

While in his final year of this course he took a mature students' university matriculation course at Park Lane College of Further Education and through the completion of both this and the miners' course he gained a full-time under-graduate place in the Faculty of Social Science, University of Glasgow.

In 1987–88, after one year's study in Glasgow, Keith gained an 'exchange' year abroad studying philosophy and politics in New York. He did voluntary work in black areas of New York and also completed an internship in the State Legislative Capital of Albany, before returning to Glasgow and completing his MA. He then took up postgraduate work and worked part-time in a number of jobs before gaining a MPhil (with distinction) in 1995 from the European Philosophical Inquiry Centre in Glasgow.

Keith now works full-time for Glasgow University's Department of Adult and Continuing Education coordinating and teaching philosophy on the Out-reach (pre-Access) programme. He teaches medical ethics and aesthetics and is particularly proud of having just completed a 'pilot' programme in St Kenneth's School, Greenock where he taught philosophy to 7-year-olds.

Keith is now researching his PhD thesis on Aristotle and the way his work on ethics relates to modern twentieth century adult education movements.

Claire S. left the Bon Sauveur Convent School, Holyhead, North Wales in July 1950, aged 16, after taking the school certificate examination, and did a year's commercial course at the then Nottingham Technical College (now Nottingham Trent University). She worked for a short time as a reporter on local papers in Derby, Morecambe and Wisbech and then worked in the Stand-ards Department at Boots Headquarters in Nottingham, during which time she took art lessons at the Nottingham College of Art. After getting married she had three children and lived in different parts of England as well as being stationed in Singapore, Malta and Germany with her serviceman husband. Returning to England in 1977, the family settled in Peterborough after her husband retired from the RAF. When he died in 1984 she decided to take an Open University course in social science and graduated with honours (third class) in 1995.

In 1993 she became a founder member of the University of the Third Age in Peterborough, having been asked to join the Steering Committee which got it off the ground. She has been a Committee member since then.

In 1995 she was a regional winner of an Adult Learners' Week award given by the National Institute of Adult Continuing Education, having been nominated by the U3A in Peterborough.

Claire continues classes with the U3A in French and German and has attended other shorter courses with the organization, including word process-ing, local history and oil painting. She has also tutored a class in art history.

Claire was Secretary for seven years of the Peterborough branch of the Child Poverty Action Group and is also Secretary of the Heltwate Community Association in Bretton, Peterborough, as well as being a member of the local Family History Society. She continues to encourage others never to finish learning.

David H.'s story is inextricably bound up with the massive changes taking place in the employment base of the North East of England. Declared redundant with the closure of the last coal mine in the Durham coalfield, David has used this as an opportunity to open up a new life for himself on the 'chalk face' of higher education.

His entry into education was the result of an initiative by Monkwearmouth College to respond to the lifelong learning needs of redundant miners, through a series of taster courses.

> Due to the closure of Wearmouth Colliery in December 1994, I enrolled part-time at Monkwearmouth College, studying basic maths, English, computing and a hitch-hiker's guide to science and technology. Whilst at College I soon realized that studying was enjoyable and nothing like school and that there were plenty of opportunities for adults to progress further in education.

David's fresh approach and sense of excitement with learning is underpinned with a sense of the practical realities of embarking on this course of action. As his College tutor notes,

> his decision to pursue a full-time course of education is a brave one, because he has a family to support, has had no formal education for many years and has chosen a course in an academically demanding area. Many people on being made redundant despair of the future. In David's case he was determined to make something of the rest of his life and, having balanced the long term prospects from education against his self-analysis of being a poor student, decided to give it a chance.

David is now following a University of Sunderland degree course in electrical and electronic engineering. Yet even though this and his family commitments are very demanding, he still finds time to contribute to the College's 'Outreach Team' and assists in supporting and advising other adults in making a choice for learning.

The University of Wales Swansea's *Community University of the Valleys* programme (CUV) is an imaginative and successful attempt to meet the needs of rapidly changing communities facing high levels of unemployment and social deprivation. Located at Banwen, a relatively isolated former coal community in the Dulais Valley, the CVU is built upon partnerships with Onllwyn Community Council, and with the locally based DOVE Workshop, a women's training organization which had grown out of the local Miners' Support Group in the year long coal strike of 1984–85.

The CUV provision, which ranges from short courses in IT and the Welsh language, to a part-time BA in Humanities, is funded by the Higher Education

Funding Council for Wales and the European Social Fund. It is located at the local Community Centre (which formerly housed offices of the National Coal Board), which was extensively refurbished in 1993, as a result of an input of funds from University of Wales Swansea, Neath Borough Council, and the European Regional Development Fund. The Centre contains teaching rooms, a purpose built library and crèche, and an IT lab.

The CUV is administered by the Department of Adult Education at University of Wales Swansea, but the University is not the exclusive provider. The DOVE Workshop acts as an education and training 'broker', and works also with the WEA and the local FE college. Over 200 students use the centre each week during term time. These various partnerships have meant that a wide portfolio of courses are available, and one of the central goals has been that of providing a variety of starting points and progression routes.

The most advanced level of provision at the CUV is that of the part-time degree in humanities. The first cohort of students enrolled on this programme at Banwen in 1993. In 1996, partnerships at undergraduate level were extended, when the Open University in Wales and the University of Glamorgan joined the scheme, which extended both the geographical area of provision, and the range of subjects and course options.

The theme of partnership is central to both the origins and ongoing practice of the CUV. Indeed it is the nature of the partnerships, with the local community and the voluntary sector, which marks off the CUV from earlier adult education provision in the area. The driving force locally has come from women; this is highly symptomatic of cultural and political changes in South Wales in recent years.

The CUV might be seen, therefore, as a modernization of the adult education tradition in South Wales. As well as providing much needed educational opportunities for individuals, it contributes, with many other agencies, to ongoing economic and social regeneration of communities, and, ultimately, to the remaking of the region as a whole. In the case of the University of Swansea at least, the CUV also plays a part in the remaking — perhaps even the modernization — of its parent institution, as it enters the post-Dearing world of higher education.

Responding to Dearing

Dearing's recommendations on diversity and widening participation, in particular as discussed in chapters 1 and 4, are all relevant here.

Part 3

Curriculum

7 Modules, Semesters and Credits

Before Robbins, the typical UK degree was an undifferentiated 'linear lump', taken full-time, in regulated sequence, and with choice confined to specialist subjects or options. Post-Robbins, and in line with his injunctions on breadth and interdisciplinarity, new subjects, combinations and pedagogical techniques became possible, as in the *vogue* within the new universities for combined honours degrees. Part-time study possibilities (with the honourable exception of 'liberal adult' and 'extension' courses discussed in chapter 8) did not really begin until the advent of the Open University in 1970. Post-Baker (if we are to believe institutional and sectoral propaganda), modularity, semesterization and the widespread adoption of credit accumulation and transfer schemes (CATs) have opened up a new world of portable credit, intermediate qualifications, and potential mixed-mode study.

A series of surveys of institutional commitment to credit recognition, to intermediate awards, to mixed modes of study, to reform of the academic year, and to student choice imply that the academic world has changed, or is about to do so. Figure 7.1 is an example, demonstrating nearly three-quarters of UK institutions committed to the kind of curriculum design implied by modularity, semesterization, credit exchange, and recognition of prior experiential learning. This is the context in which the huge summary report, *Choosing to Change* was published in 1994 (Robertson, 1994).

Institutional intentions like these have to be tested against present and future achievements. The empirical outcome is rather different, and again belies the impression of a genuinely 'mass' system.

Modular pioneers in the UK are often regarded as City Polytechnic (now London Guildhall University) and Oxford Polytechnic (now Oxford Brookes University), which have been running successful and distinctive institution-wide schemes since the early 1970s. But they, in turn, built upon influential practice elsewhere: notably in the United States, and through the Open University. Nor should this be seen just as a new university phenomenon: University of London science courses have, for example, always been organized on a unit credit basis.

The fundamental principles of modularity are simple: courses are arranged into blocks or units aggregated for an award (credit accumulation), and each unit is normally assessed upon completion (progressive assessment). To these two principles most advocates add a third; the main purpose of designing (or redesigning) a course in this way is to allow greater flexibility, responsibility and choice for students. Without this vital element a number of courses have

Figure 7.1   Survey of credit schemes in all universities, 1993

Questions	%	n
• Currently with CAT scheme • Plans to introduce scheme within three years • No plans to introduce scheme	63 21 16	48 16 12
• Membership of CAT consortia • Accept credit from consortium members = yes	40 90	36 36
• Current schemes accepting WBL, EBL or APEL	71	34
• Response rate from 88 universities	86	76

Data compiled from: Harold Harvey and Brian Norton, University of Ulster, Survey of CAT schemes in UK universities, commissioned by the Institute of Environmental Health Officers (IEHO), March 1993.

simply been repackaged, and in the process not only failed to demonstrate a clear academic rationale but also held out to students promises that they could not fulfil. In the summary report of the Oxford experience such examples were termed 'phantom modularity' (Watson et al., 1989).

Modularity, as also asserted by the Oxford authors, is a vehicle for careful course design and many of the adverse charges laid at its door (lack of coherence and progression, for example) have more to do with lack of care in setting course regulations than with the notion of credit accumulation itself. In 1996 the HEQC published an interesting series of reflections on the implementation of modularity in the UK in their 'in-focus' series. This began with a restatement of the arguments for and against the process as experienced at Oxford, reproduced below as figure 7.2 (Watson, 1996, pp. 6–9).

The remainder of the HEQC volume simply underlines how far modularity has become an ideologically contested term during the era of post-Baker expansion. As an innovation it has been regarded, quite unfairly, as synonymous with cost-cutting and loss of curricular control, springing an intense critique that, when investigated closely, is much more about the manner in which institutions, from the centre, have sought to implement the changes, than their actual and potential merits in improving the academic experience of students. Given some local economies of scale (all available for reinvestment in the academic product) and following a necessary developmental stage (during which it is essential to get management information systems right), the resource effects of running a modular rather than a traditional curriculum should be neutral.

The internal opposition has, however, allied resentment with what has happened to the resourcing and culture of higher education as a whole with this set of developments in particular. Distinguished left-wing voices within the academy have directly attacked the notion of greater freedom and choice for students and paradoxically sought to entrench a profound cultural conservatism (Rustin, 1994).

Figure 7.2 *Inventory of arguments for and against modularity*

FLEXIBILITY	
For	**Against**
Choice of courses and units; opportunities for transfer and exchange; a varied pace of study; enables students to make constant adjustments to their programmes as interests and abilities develop.	Educational objections to a wide range of choice; accusations of 'pick-and-mix' or 'cafeteria-style' courses; lack of coherence and progression when measured against conventional schemes; flexibility more apparent than real; logistical constraints, such as timetable congestion or split-site operation, thwart educational objectives.

ECONOMY	
For	**Against**
Significant economies, especially through common teaching and the resulting economy of group size; small group work, particularly with advanced students, protected even in circumstances of increasing pressure on staff-student ratios.	Economies harder to achieve in practice than in theory; inherited patterns of accommodation make large group teaching on a wide scale difficult to achieve; economies on the teaching side more than offset by the complex demands of administration and the potentially heavy demands of assessment and examination.

PROGRESSIVE ASSESSMENT	
For	**Against**
Student experience of progressive assessment influences programme choice in a healthy and constructive way; knowledge of 'how I am doing' assists students in working to their strengths, compensating for weaknesses and, most significantly, potentially revising their qualification aims on an informed and realistic basis.	Progressive assessment can lead to 'tactical' as opposed to principled choices and, as a consequence of averaging individual module marks and grades, can lead to insufficient attention to a student's final level of achievement.

CAREFUL DESIGN	
For	**Against**
In a large multi-subject environment it is important for the left hand to know what the right hand is doing. Module descriptions are written to an agreed formula: specifying relationships with other modules; including level and prerequisites, general educational aims, teaching and learning methods, breakdown of likely student hours, course content, and the assessment scheme. As public documents they are available to staff and students and susceptible to regular checks for their academic respectability, potential overlap with other modules and potential use for new programmes or fields. Significant changes are subject to public validation and recording.	Keeping course information at this level generally available is time-consuming and expensive. Public currency of this kind can also lead to conservatism in course design or 'playing safe'. The dangers of over-prescriptiveness and/or superficiality are also difficult to avoid.

Figure 7.2 (cont'd)

THE STUDENT RECORD AND TRANSCRIPT	
For	**Against**
Students completing a qualification have more authenticated information about their educational experience than other graduates or diplomates, both in terms of subjects studied and levels achieved. Strong hypothesis that the experience of negotiating a programme of study in this amount of detail, and of being able to demonstrate the outcomes to employers, explains the success of graduates in the job market.	The transcript can be read as confirming the patchiness and lack of coherence of the student's course ('islands of knowledge in a sea of ignorance'). By itself the student's termly record or final transcript cannot confirm that he or she has achieved the intellectual maturity or special skills associated with graduate status in various fields.

PUBLIC UNDERSTANDING	
For	**Against**
Modular courses tune in well with concerns that higher education should be more 'flexible', 'interchangeable', and recognize the achievements of students in non-traditional educational environments; hence the boom in schemes for credit transfer and exchange, for assessment of prior and experiential learning, for distance learning, and for the recognition of non-standard entry qualifications. The 'negotiable' framework includes opportunities for exemptions and admission with advanced standing as well as for remedial and 'balancing' study. It also allows for 'lifelong' education, especially through the use of the ladder of intermediate awards.	Public enthusiasm and endorsement, especially at the rhetorical level, should not be allowed to disguise the extent to which such courses continue to confuse groups such as employers, schools, colleges and careers advisers.

Source: Based on Watson 1989, 1996.

Post-modularity

For the university system fully to play its part in the scheme of lifelong learning it will have to get past many of these technical issues. It will, in fact, have to move through the modular to the post-modular world. This world will make use of the following elements of curriculum design: units of study; potentially portable credit; intermediate as well as major awards; individualized as well as group-customized programmes of study; and acceptance of study for personal as well as professional ends. This vision is sometimes criticized for its potential homogeneity and convergence, but it does not imply that all institutions, courses, subjects or teaching approaches need be the same. For those institutions most firmly committed to full-time, linear study of the type set out at the beginning of this chapter it should pragmatically only be necessary to identify satisfactory assessment at the end of a year's equivalent of full-time study in order to articulate with a national qualifications framework. All institutions will, however, have to be more explicit about objectives, outcomes and standards, and to enable the academic community of teachers and students as well as their external sponsors to understand what credit and its accumulation into awards really means.

The Dearing 'framework of qualifications', set out below as figure 7.3 could play a major role in achieving this objective.

If universally (or indeed only widely) adopted, the Dearing framework has the capacity simultaneously to solve (or at least alleviate) several related problems:

1   it offers a general benchmark for credit points without imposing a universal module or unit size;

2   it binds together traditional qualification titles (adding a new one — see below) and the levels specified for National Vocational Qualifications (NVQs);

3   it tackles the specific problem of the articulation of the 'higher national' awards (HNCs and HNDs), by making the 'certificate' award a specific stage towards the 'diploma' (as in Scotland; in England it is generally used at present to denote a part-time version of the diploma award);

4   it also tackles the relatively anarchic situation whereby certain subjects (usually in collusion with professional bodies) have developed longer undergraduate honours degrees and (mis)appropriated the 'masters' title to describe them — these become 'higher honours' at level 5;

5   also at level 5 the framework rolls back the misleading description (largely adopted for marketing purposes) of the masters title for courses designed to equip graduates of one discipline to operate as graduates in another (as also discussed in the HEFCE, CVCP and SCOP, *Review of Postgraduate Education*) (Harris, 1996);

6   it specifically addresses the issue of 'specific' vs. 'general' credit — awards are not earned, or entry to higher levels secured, on the basis of accumulation of credit points alone — the admitting or awarding institution has to recognize enough credit with the appropriate content to confirm admission, progress or qualification;

7   similarly, there is acknowledgment that courses and students' profiles of achievement will vary in terms of breadth and specialization (see chapter 8) and can be adjusted (through both 'acceleration' and 'deceleration') to prepare for specific awards;

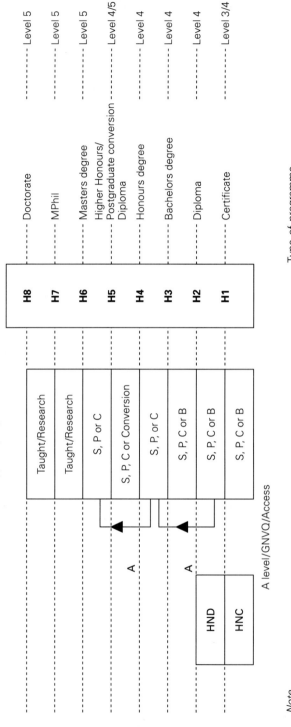

Figure 7.3 Dearing: A qualifications framework

Type of programme	Level	Qualification Title	NVQ
Taught/Research	H8	Doctorate	Level 5
Taught/Research	H7	MPhil	Level 5
S, P or C	H6	Masters degree	Level 5
S, P, C or Conversion	H5	Higher Honours/ Postgraduate conversion Diploma	Level 4/5
S, P, or C	H4	Honours degree	Level 4
S, P, C or B	H3	Bachelors degree	Level 4
S, P, C or B	H2	Diploma	Level 4
S, P, C or B	H1	Certificate	Level 3/4

HND

HNC

A level/GNVQ/Access

Type of programme

A = Accelerated route if correct number of specialist credit points acquired
S = Single subject
C = Combined subjects
B = Broad range of subjects
P = Subject leading to professional status
Conversion = Postgraduate conversion course

Note
1 Each level up to H4 would require at least 120 additional credit points.
2 Students pursuing broad programmes at levels H1, H2 and H3 and securing 360 credit points would be awarded a Bachelors degree.
3 To achieve an honours degree would require at least 360 specialist credit points. The rate of progress would depend on the amount of previous specialization.
4 It would be for each institution, consulting as appropriate with professional bodies, to determine the pattern of credits (for example, how much specialization or how much breadth) required to qualify for an honours degree.
Source: NCIHE, 1997, Summary Report, p. 18.

8 finally, it is noted that when Scotland (for which the Scottish Com-
    mittee recommended a slightly different framework, but on the same
    principles) has clarified the funding and articulation of the final year
    of secondary school and the first year of university education, there is
    a basis here for a fully national system of awards (NCIHE, 1997, Report
    of the Scottish Committee, Chart 4.2).

Above all the framework makes the considerable conceptual advance of
being designed more like a climbing-frame than a ladder. It is assumed that
not all students' progress will be linear, even or unbroken. 'Intermediate' awards
should have real currency (the 'standards' issues discussed in chapter 11 are of
vital importance here); students may wish to move back one or more levels to
develop new knowledge and skills pathways; and the prospects of employer
and public understanding of awards will be improved.

Responding to Dearing

Dearing's recommendations in this area are all in the direction of reducing discrimination between different modes of study and facilitating flexible use of the new qualifications framework. Early evaluation suggests
that they go further in this second respect (especially in the emphasis on
the 'Progress File' and on the specification of programme outcomes), than
in the former, where the failure to grasp the full implications of funding
students and institutions in a manner that is agnostic as to mode gives the
impression of tinkering rather than of root-and-branch reform.

*We recommend that institutions of higher education, over the medium term,
develop a Progress File. The File should consist of two elements:*

- *a transcript recording student achievement which should follow a
  common format devised by institutions collectively through their representative bodies;*

- *a means by which students can monitor, build and reflect upon their
  personal development (recommendation 20).*

*We recommend that institutions of higher education begin immediately to
develop, for each programme they offer, a 'programme specification' which
identifies potential stopping-off points and gives the intended outcomes of the
programme in terms of:*

- *the knowledge and understanding that a student will be expected to
  have upon completion;*

- *key skills: communication, numeracy, the use of information techno-logy and learning how to learn;*

- *cognitive skills, such as an understanding of methodologies or ability in critical analysis;*

- *subject specific skills, such as laboratory skills (recommendation 21).*

We recommend that the government, the representative bodies, the Quality Assurance Agency, other awarding bodies and the organizations which over-see them, should endorse immediately the framework for higher education qualifications that we have proposed (recommendation 22).

Like many other aspects of the Dearing Report, this bundle of recom-mendations will require concerted commitment and coordinated action on a number of fronts if the objectives are to be achieved:

1. from the government in terms of the development of funding policies and the review of social security so that students can achieve optimum benefit from a national system of articulated awards (discussed in chapter 12);
2. from the institutions individually in devising the 'programme specifications', adhering to the 'qualifications framework', and facilitating the 'progress file';
3. from the institutions collectively in supporting the relevant devel-opmental agenda of the proposed Institute for Learning and Teach-ing (ILT) (see also chapters 8 and 14) and the Quality Assurance Agency (QAA); and
4. from the staff of the relevant agencies in meeting unprecedented challenges on a sector-wide scale.

At the theoretical level these are commitments that previous statements of policy and intent suggest should be relatively easy to endorse. The way forward is, however, likely to be rocky. Dearing has already 'trimmed' expectations in respect of support of part-time students. Institutions will have to face both a heavy body of description (ideally redescription) of course objectives and students, as well as the uncomfortable prospect of withdrawing inadequate or misleading course titles. Meanwhile the two key agencies are in one case (QAA) still on the drawing-board and in the other (ILT) significantly untried and untested.

8   Learning in the University

This chapter focuses on the historical cultures of learning in the British university, and particularly a perceived struggle for supremacy between teaching and research. Dearing attempts to redraw the battle-lines, in particular through an emphasis on learning rather than teaching, although he maintains a traditional view of the contribution of scholarship to high quality taught programmes.

The Map of Knowledge

The authors of the Dearing Report are committed to a view of the distinctive features of learning and teaching in higher education, invoking conventional ideas about the development of understanding, of the ability to apply knowledge in a variety of contexts, and above all about the capacity of students to join in 'learning conversations' with their tutors and their peers. These 'conversations' depend critically upon 'common understanding of terms, assumption, questions, modes of argument, and the body of evidence' (NCIHE, 1997, Main Report 8.6).

Such an approach acknowledges the fluidity of academic interests and the focus of inquiry, and Dearing tries at several points to take the side of new and interdisciplinary projects against the rigidities of canons and disciplines. A similar line of inquiry leads to an endorsement of Robbins' often-forgotten plea for breadth in curricula and courses — a theme strongly endorsed by the Scottish Committee in their defence of the Scottish 'general' three-year degree, and extended (four-year) honours degree (NCIHE, 1997, Main Report 9.7).

Higher education has always been exposed to the challenge of new subjects, often emerging in the gaps between disciplines, and problem-solving approaches which necessitate interdisciplinarity. More recently these challenges have been compounded by an emerging epistemology to which traditional disciplinary boundaries make decreasing sense. This new thrust is not simply based in post-modernist thinking, with its emphasis on contextual relativity, although it is often collapsed into a general charge against 'post-modernity' by those chiefly threatened by it (Smith and Webster, 1997). The set of revised epistemological commitments to which we refer is best captured by Michael Gibbons and his collaborators in their influential collection of essays on *The New Production of Knowledge* (Gibbons et al., 1994).

Briefly, Gibbons et al. describe a paradigm shift from what they call scientific knowledge 'mode 1' to 'mode 2':

in mode 1 problems are set and solved in a context governed by the, largely academic, interests of a specific community. By contrast, mode 2 knowledge is carried out in a context of application. Mode 1 is disciplinary while mode 2 is transdisciplinary. Mode 1 is characterized by homogeneity, mode 2 by heterogeneity. Organizationally, mode 1 is hierarchical and tends to preserve its form, while mode 2 is more heterarchical and transient. Each employs a different type of quality control. In comparison with mode 1, mode 2 is more socially accountable and reflexive. (ibid., p. 3)

One of the group, Peter Scott, describes some of the implications for the university:

... while mode 1 was linear and cumulative with (pure) science as the ultimate source of innovation, mode 2 is multivariant and even anti-coherent. The source of innovation is to be found not only, or even especially, in the laboratory. It is just as likely to occur in the dynamics of the marketplace or in larger socioeconomic or cultural transformations. Indeed, it is most likely to arise in the often contested borderland between the university and the market/society. (Scott, 1995, p. 144)

This is a complex proposition and Scott goes on to explain how many of the more 'open' features of mode 2 knowledge were characteristic of professional inquiry before seventeenth century science captured the institutional heartland. For our purposes here its chief significance is the way in which it potentially extends the 'curriculum conversation' (supplementing the conventional 'learning conversation') to include key stake-holders outside the academy (Bocock and Watson, 1994, pp. 129–37).

Knowledge and Skills

A special angle on the development of knowledge and skills is provided by the 'competence' movement advanced by the supporters of national vocational qualifications like the National Council for Vocational Qualifications (NCVQ), although as Ronald Barnett and others have pointed out 'operational' competence, or 'performative' skill, is quite different from 'academic' competence (or 'deep initiation into forms of thought' as well as 'forms of life') (Barnett, 1997a, p. 37).

Through an influential series of interventions, Barnett has advanced the proposition that 'higher' education possesses an essence which is different from and in some senses exclusive of the priorities of other levels and types of educational endeavour (Barnett, 1990, 1994, 1997b). We broadly support this conclusion, as does the Dearing Committee in the particular way sketched out above. It is significant that the 'qualifications framework' (see figure 7.3 in chapter 7 above) deliberately calibrates traditional award titles, credit points and National Vocational Qualification (NVQ) levels thereby accepting the principle of dual, or even multiple outcomes from particular courses. But we also see maintaining some academic commitments — especially to critical self-reflection — as wholly compatible with both the expansion of access and the diversification of the curriculum from within higher education (Watson, forthcoming).

The history of NVQs within higher education has been a somewhat tortured one, although there is now general acceptance of awards at levels 4 and 5 constituting an important part of the HE portfolio. Along the way tensions have arisen from the apparently rigid identification of occupational sector groups as the awarding bodies, difficulties over calibration of assessment, and even a residual fear that national standards are the thin end of a wedge opening up a national curriculum in higher education. Over time, however, a more mature understanding on both sides (the NCVQ and the institutions) has emerged as has an appropriate balance between competence/skill and knowledge/understanding in HE vocational qualifications.

Against the background of this uneasy, but stable, accommodation it is significant that the Dearing Committee endorses the sector's almost unanimous response to a recent government consultation, that General National Vocational Qualifications (GNVQs) should not be extended to the higher levels (4 and 5). The most telling argument in favour of this restriction is the general development of key and core skills (see also chapter 10) throughout higher education (NCIHE, 1997, Main Report 10.27).

Innovation in Teaching

What discussion of several of these developing features of the academic landscape exposes is how far critical attention to methods, techniques and values in teaching have fallen behind the research agenda. Many reasons have been put forward for this, including the superior role of research in personal and institutional reputational terms, in reward structures, and in intrinsic interest for traditional academics. At a deeper level this priority reflects the traditional sense of higher education as a form of social reproduction, with its assumption of leading-edge researchers initiating a cadre of bright 18–21-year-olds into the mysteries of disciplines, usually in an intimate 'tutorial' setting.

The evidence is that the priority of research is an international issue, and certainly the literature outside the UK is as studded with attempts to redress the balance as seen in the evidence put before Dearing by the funding councils and others. See, for example the two reports to the US academic community from the Carnegie Foundation: *Scholarship Reconsidered* (1990) and *Scholarship Assessed* (1997). In responding to the latest inquiry only 28 per cent of US universities and colleges had established centres or units for teaching improvement (Boyer, 1990; Huber et al., 1997).

While there is no definitive parallel survey in the UK, our impression is that the performance of the UK higher sector would be considerably stronger in this respect. Part of the reason for this is historical, especially with the influence of the CNAA, which clearly extended beyond that part of the system in which it held validation and awarding authority. Other beneficial influences have been a set of official and informal agencies, relating to the sector on either a subscription or a project basis: UCOSDA, 'Education for Capability', the HEQC's 'enhancement' division, the Open Learning Foundation etc. A lively and innovative sub-culture exists within and between higher education institutions, spawning a huge volume of grey literature and innovative ideas. However, its impact on the research-led institution is variable and in general slight.

Dearing not only supports such developments but also urges the foundation of an Institute for Teaching and Learning designed to bring together in an efficient and authoritative way the various agencies and interest groups that currently separately (and often competitively) attempt to enhance teaching and learning across the sector. The implicit agenda is to inspire a new pedagogy, both more professional and reflective, and more pluralistic in its approach, in order to meet the needs of a more heterogeneous as well as a larger student body. The Dearing Committee would like the outcomes to be explicitly 'world-class' (NCIHE, 1997, Main Report 8.76).

The Role of Communications and Information Technology

For a substantial but influential minority of commentators on higher education, it is computers and information technology that will solve both of the major problems alluded to above: teaching quality and curriculum development in a mass system. Frank Webster and Kevin Robins have memorably referred to this as the theory of the 'technological fix' (Webster and Robins, 1989). Dearing is more circumspect but none the less enthusiastic about the role which communications and information technology (particularly) the former should play.

The choice of the rather old-fashioned formulation 'Communications and Information Technology' (C and IT) in the Dearing Report is deliberate. The UK leadership and strategic advantage is seen much more in terms of the successful development of communications technology (especially the national network systems of JANET and SuperJANET as well as local and metropolitan area networks) than in the successful record of information technology products for teaching and learning. The substantial top-slicing of grant required to maintain the infrastructure managed by the Joint Information Systems Committee (JISC) is one of the few examples of system-wide support for a coordinated initiative. There have also been several joint initiatives in the latter area — notably the funding councils' collaboration on the Teaching and Learning Technology Programme (TLTP) — and a well-reviewed national report by Alistair MacFarlane, Principal of Heriot-Watt University, but so far little evidence of significant take-up of collaboratively designed products (HEFCE, 1996b; MacFarlane, 1992).

The reasons for the delayed advent of IT-based teaching are various: the traditional commitment of British academics to personal curriculum design at all levels, including the introductory (a variant on the 'not invented here' syndrome); the very high production values, cost and lead-times associated with Open University materials as a brand leader; and, with honourable exceptions (such as the take-up by pharmacy departments of materials that remove the need for animal experimentation), the lack of interest of subject and professional associations. None the less, as Dearing underlines, a combination of technological development and the increased preparedness and comfort of students with the C and IT environment, will make this more a top priority for future professional development in teaching.

A parallel positive incentive will come from increased competition in the distance-learning market, especially from North America. Although there are still significant hurdles to overcome — including the cultural specificity of much course material, the problems of security of access and protection of intellectual property, and the continuing desire of students for the intimacy of face-to-face contact with teachers and full membership of an academic institution — the prospects for global delivery of curriculum and courses are immediate (as discussed below in chapter 16).

Research

As this account underlines, research has traditionally, although rather uncritically, been regarded as a necessary 'environmental' feature of higher education. Teaching at this level, the argument goes, cannot be accomplished without the direct contribution of researchers and (rather more vaguely) the 'atmosphere' of research. This assumption was seriously questioned both before and during the post-Baker expansion, leading for example to calls for a hierarchy of institutions: research-led, teaching only, and mixed (R, T and X). The cases for and against this proposition tended to be exclusively economic: 'we can't afford every institution to do high quality research' vs. 'we must afford universal research support'.

Interestingly, the Dearing Inquiry sides more with the traditional than the neo-utilitarian view. 'Scholarship' in support of teaching is identified as one of the five separate strands of research, and deserving of its own dedicated funding (see chapter 13). This has an overt political motivation: to protect and give due status to those universities whose priority is to provide teaching and learning of high quality.

Responding to Dearing

Dearing brings together several themes in attempting to address these dilemmas:

1   the notion of explicit professionalism in teaching (see also chapter 14);

> 2 collaborative approaches to curriculum development (especially involving communications and information technology [CIT]), along with a recommendation that all students should be 'connected', at home and in the university;
> 3 an echo of Robbins in a renewed call for breadth and interdisciplinarity, but allied with a more explicit recognition of preparation for work;
> 4 adjustments to the approaches to both research training and research assessment in the same vein.

The key relevant recommendations are as follows:

We recommend that, with immediate effect, all institutions of higher education give high priority to developing and implementing learning and teaching strategies which focus on the promotion of students' learning (recommendation 8).

We recommend that the representative bodies, in consultation with the funding bodies, should immediately establish a professional Institute for Learning and Teaching in Higher Education. The functions of the Institute would be to accredit programmes of training for higher education teachers; to commission research and development in learning and teaching practices; and to stimulate innovation (recommendation 14).

We recommend that the Institute should:

- *develop, over the medium term, a system of kitemarking to identify good computer-based learning materials;*

- *coordinate the national development, over the medium and long term, of computer-based learning materials, and manage initiatives to develop such materials;*

- *facilitate discussion between all relevant interest groups on promoting the development of computer-based materials to provide common units or modules, particularly for the early undergraduate years (recommendation 15).*

We recommend that all institutions of higher education should, over the medium term, review the programmes they offer:

- *with a view to securing a better balance between breadth and depth across programmes than currently exists;*

- *so that all undergraduate programmes include sufficient breadth to enable specialists to understand their specialism within its context (recommendation 16).*

We recommend to institutions of higher education that they should, over the next two years, review their postgraduate research training to ensure that they include, in addition to understanding of a range of research methods and training in appropriate technical skills, the development of professional skills, such as communication, self-management and planning (recommendation 31).

We recommend that the funding bodies and the research councils commission a study to evaluate the funding of interdisciplinary research, including the incentives and disincentives. The report should be ready to inform the next Research Assessment Exercise (recommendation 32).

We recommend to the funding bodies that, in the interests of transparency and applying international standards properly, the practice of including one or more international members in all Research Assessment Exercise (RAE) panels, wherever possible, should be introduced to the next RAE (recommendation 33).

We recommend to higher education institutions that they consider the scope for encouraging entrepreneurship through innovative approaches to programme design and through specialist postgraduate programmes (recommendation 40).

We recommend that by 2000/01 higher education institutions should ensure that all students have open access to a Networked Desktop Computer, and expect that by 2005/06 all students will be required to have access to their own portable computer (recommendation 46).

In principle there should be little opposition, and much approbation, for this set of items, although it will be interesting to see if Dearing's injunctions on breadth, interdisciplinarity and the role of what is now called entrepreneurship fare any better than the same ideas in Robbins.

Establishing the Institute of Learning and Teaching will require a considerable collective effort, as will cooperation on the preparation of IT-based teaching materials (we discuss below, in chapter 14, its potential impact on the regulation of the profession). The issue of student access to computer network poses questions about resources (including the extent to which purchase of portable computers is subsidized or coordinated for bulk purchase) but goes with the grain of well-established developments.

9   Learning Away from the University

Informal learning in the post-compulsory sector has always been on a large scale. The numbers of adult students studying part-time through extra-mural provision, for example, were always far greater in the 1960s and 1970s than the number of full-time undergraduate students: and when the picture is broadened to include the whole post-compulsory sector, the contrast was even more marked. By 1995–96 there were over three million learners in the FE sector alone (FEFC, 1996).

The 'Extra-mural' Tradition

In this context, however, there was always a clear demarcation between the 'extra-mural' and the mainstream. There were extra-mural certificates and the like, though even these were for a minority of courses, and many adult education practitioners, particularly those from a Workers Educational Association (WEA) background, regarded with suspicion any form of certification. The predominant culture of the extra-mural tradition was characterized by two concepts: learning for learning's sake, and learning for social purpose. In neither context was there much room for certification (the assignment of credit): the first stressed the importance of personal development and the sheer joy of learning, and the second the wider social and political goals of emancipation and empowerment through the acquisition of knowledge and understanding (see Wallis, 1995; and Taylor et al., 1985).

There were, of course, contact points between the worlds of adult education and the university mainstream. Some University Extension Certificates were validated by the parent university as being at general degree standard although over a narrower range of subject matter. For example, the University of Leeds introduced University Extension Certificates in a range of subjects and these were provided successfully for adult students from the 1950s to the 1980s. Other universities, most notably London, Hull, Nottingham and Sheffield, offered similar schemes. In an *ad hoc* way, typical of the British system, some adult students were granted 'advanced standing' onto undergraduate degree courses as a result of their extra-mural study; and significant numbers of others were able to use their extra-mural study as a means to gain entry to the university.

But these were all very marginal activities. Not until the beginning of the rapid expansion of higher education, and the creation of the polytechnics, was there policy-led integration of the formal higher education system and the informal learning characterized by its adult and part-time nature.

The heralded transition from an elite to a mass system of higher education demonstrated, amongst many other things, that the traditional elite university system had no monopoly of learning and knowledge. The assumptions both of exclusivity and of rigid boundaries were shown to be false. In every aspect advocates of a mass system have challenged both conceptually and practically these assumptions. As indicated in chapter 1, the majority of students in higher education are now over 21, and an increasing number part-time and locally based. The subjects studied now include a wide range of vocational and professionally related areas which are neither disciplinary nor knowledge-based in the conventional sense. The awards for which students are registered extend far beyond the conventional three-year full-time honours degree.

Of course, many of these new patterns — and the modularity and credit-based structures which accompany them — apply far more to the new than to the traditional university sector. There is unparalleled diversity in the system. But, as Peter Scott has noted, the key points about the new system are its 'fuzziness and permeability' (Scott, 1995, p. 169). Higher education is characterized by its lack of clear definition, organizationally, epistemologically and culturally, and its increasing interaction with and interdependence upon a range of 'external' agencies and actual or potential partners.

Having changed from an elite to the prospects of a mass model of higher education it is now clear that the 'permeability' of the new system can lead to a much broader 'learning society . . . (embracing) education and training in non-educational settings — in the so-called "corporate classroom" in industry and business, within the community and voluntary organizations, through the mass media, along the information technology super-highways, in the context of Total Quality Management and Investors In People' (ibid., p. 32).

To facilitate high quality learning in this new learning society raises both organizational (or technical) and epistemological questions. The former are easier to describe and indeed to deal with. They fall under two main heads: modes of delivery and methods of assessment. The most obvious and important point about modes of delivery is the impact of the computing revolution on higher education.

IT and Distance Learning

The changes in university learning as a result of computer-based learning are already profound, but in future they could revolutionize learning through creating off-campus, distance learning opportunities on a national and international basis. The contexts and motivations for such learning are extremely varied, as the Open University has already shown: from learning in the home via PC and television and primarily for personal development, through to learning in the workplace primarily for career advancement.

Such developments raise the obvious possibility of the non-campus university — the replication of the model of the Milton Keynes, Open University (or Athabasca Distance Learning University in Alberta, Canada and any number of other, national 'open universities'). There are numerous possible variations on this model, with greater or lesser degrees of staff/student contact time, concentrated or very long-term periods of study for awards, and so on. But the potential for a totally different type of university system, knowing no geographical boundaries and catering for the full range of students in terms of age, motivations and general orientation, is now technologically realizable.

This immediately shades into epistemological or more generally cultural questions. Does the university 'learning experience' necessarily involve the physical campus and if so why? Does the pedagogy of higher education — critical thinking, staff/student intellectual interchange, and the rest — depend necessarily upon face-to-face learning contexts?

There are also other organizational issues to consider. Traditionally, the British system of higher education has had high and narrow entry standards — defined normally by good 'A' level or Scottish Higher grades — and high retention and success rates. Intelligent 18-year-olds, well socialized into the disciplinary knowledge base of their subjects and well versed in traditional working methods in higher education and in examination techniques, have usually needed only 'light touch' teaching.

All this has changed, in virtually all universities, though with enormous variations across the system. Not only have entry qualifications become much more varied — Access courses, BTEC, NVQ and GNVQ et al. — the much wider questions of accrediting relevant experience are also being raised. Accreditation of Prior Learning (APL) and Accreditation of Prior Experiential Learning (APEL) are becoming increasingly important mechanisms for students at all levels, particularly mature students with both work and life experience. Many universities now provide credit-bearing AP(E)L modules which facilitate students codifying their experience and matching it to the academic requirements of the curriculum. In some cases this can provide advanced standing through exemption from studying particular aspects of the curriculum — a process made much easier within a modularized structure; in other cases the AP(E)L process itself can form the basis of individually-designed learning programmes, prepared jointly by the student and the university.

Learning in the Workplace

A particularly striking example of the latter process has been the rapid development of Work-Based Learning (WBL) programmes whereby, on a variety of models, employees and companies work in partnership with the university to provide integrated programmes, incorporating AP(E)L and addressing both work-related and academic areas within the context of a quality-assured university award. (The National Centre for Workbased Learning Partnerships, based at Middlesex University, provides publications describing these developments, and a journal *The Workbased Learning Bulletin* is also edited from the University.) These processes can involve the accreditation of in-company training provision, the preparation and supervision by the company, albeit in conjunction with the university, of project work in the learning package, and of course substantial AP(E)L elements. Much of the learning can also be experienced on-line through computer-based links between the university and the company concerned, and the award completed on a very flexible timescale. Although at present in the UK most WBL provision is locally and regionally based, and is fairly small scale, the potential is high and is international in scope (with several transnational organizations now committed to the 'corporate classroom'). Several new universities — Middlesex, Portsmouth and Staffordshire among others — have quite extensive and innovative WBL programmes. Some of the traditional universities are also beginning to develop work in this area, especially at post-graduate levels.

As indicated above, all this raises large epistemological questions. How is learning and knowledge in higher education defined, delineated and validated? In the past, there was a normally unstated assumption that the university defined and set standards for higher education, that the university system was self-regulatory and that, within the system, the core academic disciplines and their methodologies formed the kernel of what we would now term quality assurance. As has been well-rehearsed by many analysts and commentators, 'academic' as opposed to 'vocational and applied' knowledge has always been regarded within British education, and within the wider culture, as being superior (see, for example, Roderick and Stephens, 1982). This has permeated at a fundamental level our whole system: grammar schools, universities, the primacy and status of finance capital and professional occupations (as opposed to technological and 'applied' occupations), all bear witness to this.

But again this is changing, at least to an extent. The emphases in higher education upon transferable, generic skills and upon increasingly vocationally oriented curricula discussed in chapter 8 have taken place within a context of wider social and economic change in which the place of learning and higher education generally has changed markedly. Whereas a graduate qualification from the elite system was an important element in guaranteeing high status, and usually secure and well-paid employment, the trend in the mass higher education system is towards 'the development of a "college culture" for the majority — from life chances to life styles, mirroring the larger shift towards post-industrialism' (Scott, 1995, p. 113).

An indication of the priority now being given to the provision and development of work-related learning is the new Labour government's proposal for a University for Industry (UfI). The eventual configuration of the 'University' is currently (late 1997) under active discussion but several key facets are already clear. It is to have a cross-sectoral function and is intended to spearhead a new skills revolution. There will be no separate institutional basis for provision, leaving the core function as national networking, in order to extend learning to the workplace, the home and local learning centres (Hillman, 1996). One implication will be to shift significant responsibility for training and learning from the employer to the employee, financing the initiative through a public/ private sector partnership, and making full use of both institutions' curriculum and pedagogic expertise and of the new opportunities for learning afforded by information technology.

The government's consistent emphasis upon the interrelationship between skills, economic success and social cohesion underpins the concept of the University for Industry. It is one very significant development in the paradigm shift to lifelong learning on which the Dearing Report, and government policy on post-compulsory education, are major influences. The Committee expressed its support, with significant reservations about the title (NCIHE, 1997, Main Report 16.38). The extent of universities' involvement in the UfI is not yet clear, but it provides a major opportunity for CE specialists — particularly those in the CVE area — to extend their work-related provision and their partnerships with employers.

External Influences on the Curriculum

Defining the knowledge and learning 'appropriate to a university' is no longer the exclusive preserve of the universities themselves. Several other agencies are involved — government, employers, professional bodies and, not least, the students themselves. Modularity and credit systems are breaking down the old disciplinary empires, but this challenge is also the result of the ideological pressure from these external forces. Academic curricula and concerns need to reflect the realities of the external world. Thus inter-disciplinary, problem or area based studies are often seen as much more relevant than university-defined single disciplinary areas.

In many ways, the ideological and cultural traditions of informal learning are thus informing the new world of potential mass higher education. Adult education has always had to, and indeed wanted to, respond to student per-spectives and to external partners. It has also had little regard to the inflexibilities of disciplinary boundaries. Cultural studies, and to an extent industrial studies and regional studies, for example, had their origins in adult education provi-sion. Perhaps more significantly, the general trend within mass systems is to concentrate less upon knowledge-based, disciplinary expertise and rather more upon vocationalism on the one hand and the development of generic skills on the other. Again, this represents in part a return to the culture of the informal learning environment and an acknowledgment both that the university does not exist in a social vacuum and that it no longer has, if it ever did, the monopoly on the definition and ownership of the learning process in higher education. If universities retreat into defensive mode and try to retain their pre-existing structures and cultures, they may be overtaken by the larger forces of the learning society. If they adapt to and work in partnership with the new agencies of lifelong learning development then they may become centrally important agencies of change and development. Of course, this latter path has considerable political dangers, not least the possible erosion of university autonomy, and a downgrading or even disappearance of critical thinking and some commitment to social purpose, as vocational and instrumental pressures increase and as 'credentialism' threatens to undermine liberal educational objectives.

Responding to Dearing

In addressing these points, the Dearing Report focuses especially on the role of work experience:

We recommend that the government, with immediate effect, works with representative employer and professional organizations to encourage employers to offer more work experience opportunities for students (recommendation 19).

This specific recommendation potentially exposes a gap between the theoretical commitment and the practical performance of employers (as further discussed in chapter 17). Beyond this, Dearing relies on the market — for continuous professional development as well as higher education for personal enrichment — to influence universities to modify their modes of delivery and extend their patterns of outreach. Such progress may, however, depend significantly on funding reforms, especially the incentives to employers as well as potential students to participate. In the wider context of informal learning, support for part-time study is also especially relevant.

10   The Professional Dimension

One internationally confirmed response to growth in opportunities in higher education is a greater demand for and take-up of more explicitly work-related courses. Figure 10.1 shows the pattern of choice of subject by applicants to UK higher education as it has changed over the decade 1983–94. During a period in which undergraduate numbers went up by 70 per cent the above average increases were all in professional and vocational areas, notably the professions allied to medicine (largely as a result of an NHS policy change, bringing nursing and midwifery as well as the other PAMs into HEIs), business and financial studies and information sciences. On this scale traditional engineering and science slipped back, along with languages and humanities. The apparent strong demand for multi-subject and multi-disciplinary choices appears to hold out hope for some of Dearing's vision of future breadth but it is important to note that many of these are second or 'insurance' choices.

An obvious extrapolation of this data is that as students are required to contribute more to the costs of their higher education, as they enter a potentially more competitive job market, and as the more they earn the quicker they can clear their debts, they are more likely to take instrumental options. This in turn raises issues about higher education as professional and vocational preparation, as well about its career-long role through continuing professional development (CPD) and CVE.

Professional and Vocational Higher Education

This phenomenon should not, however, be allowed to disguise the long tradition of UK professional higher education in the traditional disciplines usually associated with the traditional universities (law, medicine and theology) and the 'mainstream' technological and professional heritage of the polytechnics and the new universities.

A special success of the latter has been their achievement in bringing together academic and professional values. This has especially involved dialogue between academic teams and professional and statutory bodies, not only in terms of curriculum development, but also for the purposes of professional recognition and licence to practice. Figure 10.2 is derived from a study of professional higher education and demonstrates the points of potential convergence and divergence. Ironically it is frequently the 'academic' members of professional institutions and their relevant committees who promote the most conservative priorities. There are many instances of them working both sides

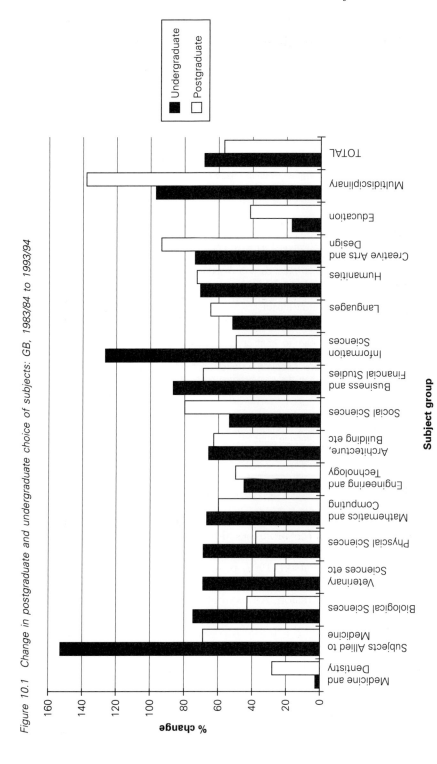

Figure 10.1 Change in postgraduate and undergraduate choice of subjects: GB, 1983/84 to 1993/94

Source: IES, 1996.

Figure 10.2   Professional body and educational concerns

- **Entry requirements**

Either party might have more or less flexible approaches to the necessary pre-course experience and qualifications of students. In general the development of more generous approaches to entry requirement by colleges, recognizing non-standard qualification and prior experiential learning, as well as an emphasis on the 'value added' by educational process, have not been fully matched by professional bodies. The latter frequently express concern about the possible impact on exit standards.

- **Cohort progression/identity**

Following the notion of professional socialization, professional bodies again tend to be more conservative about the impact of varied pace or mode of study, the possibility of late or deferred choice of routes of study leading to professional qualifications, and the impact of intending professionals and those studying for more general educational measures working together.

- **Inculcating the culture**

Claims about the general educational aims of courses invariably tend to be larger (and vaguer) than those of professional training (although this may be changing as a consequence of new models of professional practice and responsibility). Conversely, the professions may complain if the courses taken by their new members have not taken the time or trouble to inculcate aspects of working practice or assumptions (or may indeed have gone out of their way to be critical of these).

- **Exit standards**

In the extreme, this may lead to conflicting views about what the initially qualified professional values, knows, and/or is able to perform. To take a crude example, the educationalist may have greater faith in the transferability from one task to another of the skills he or she has taught than the professional body obliged to licence and indemnify.

- **Labour supply**

Another motive for professional bodies to control the exit from courses of qualified personnel is their interest variously in increasing or restricting the supply. Protectionism of this kind is much harder to sustain in educational institutions where courses are in general open to all who can achieve the requisite support (fees and maintenance) and who can benefit, intellectually or personally.

Source: Based upon Bines and Watson, 1992.

of the street, telling either the professional body or the university that one will in no circumstances tolerate what the other would like to do (for example on modularity) (Bines and Watson, 1992, p. 4).

Tensions of these kinds have always been present and in some cases have been exacerbated by expansion. An example, currently coming to a head, is the tussle between HEIs and the Engineering Council over the latter's revisions to the policy document *Standards and Routes to Registration* (SARTOR), which was adopted finally in September 1997 (Engineering Council, 1997b). The proposed scheme was intended to tighten entry qualifications to courses (measured by 'A' level points) and the so-called 'benchmark' routes to different levels of professional recognition: Chartered Engineer (CEng), Incorporated Engineer (IEng), and Engineering Technician (EngTech). Much of the language in which the proposals were promoted and initially discussed was profoundly hostile to widened access, questioned standards on courses in different types of institution, and expressed concern about the potential decline in status of the higher levels of membership. Academic institutions defended their use of alternative entry routes (besides 'A' level) and protested their ability to get non-standard entrants up to appropriate diploma and degree standards. The engineering bodies responded that they were uncertain about 'exit standards' set by universities and colleges, and unless and until such standards were secure they would have to rely on entry standards, thus rejecting the 'value-added' arguments.

Meanwhile, given the 'softness' of demand for engineering and applied science courses (directly correlated with the relatively weak collective performance of school-leavers in science and mathematics), and the 'ring-fenced' protection of engineering, computing and mathematics courses by the funding councils (which, until 1997–98, have not allowed institutions to vire places away from these subjects into those for which there is more secure demand), institutions at the lower end of the applications pecking-order are feeling highly insecure.

In at least one respect, this story is profoundly relevant to lifelong learning and continuing education. Because of the decline in post-16 schools' performance in maths and science, many of the most successful students in HE engineering and technology are a special type of 'adult returner', who have overcome their difficulties in school through the BTEC/SCOTVEC route supplied by the HNC and HND, often initially on day-release. The disdain of the Engineering Council for this honourable form of *repêchage* indicates how many of the arguments are social as well as academic.

The outcome of this particular controversy has all the air of a grudging compromise, with the Engineering Council's statement confirming their hopes, in due course, for secure output standards, 'ramping in' (over three years) the tougher entry standards, allowing a proportion of non-standard cases, and offering the Council's own Part 1 exam as an alternative accreditation at the end of year 1 for those institutions finding difficulty with the 'A' level threshold (Engineering Council, 1997b). Interestingly, the Dearing Report intervenes in this debate, by suggesting that if its recommendations for output standards at level H1 were met in this case, they could provide an alternative to SARTOR tightening entry requirements (NCIHE, 1997, Main Report 10.65).

Course Length, Quality and 'Entitlement'

As the array of professional courses in higher education has become more complex, questions about who pays for professional formation also become muddied. In cases where the funding councils have traditionally supported numbers, such as medicine, there are complex issues about the contribution of the Health Service through clinical salaries and the funding of teaching hospitals. However, the student, supported by the state over a longer period, is as generously treated as any other undergraduate in the initial phase of his or her training. This is broadly the picture for other professional courses like architecture (where the support currently runs through the five years in university required for the Diploma in Architecture) and law (where Part 1 of the Law Society requirements can be covered on a grant but not Part 2). Needless to say, the prospective personal 'rates of return' to successful individuals vary across these professional courses and between them and non-vocational courses.

In some other cases — notably the professions allied to medicine — another agency (in this case the NHS) purchases blocks of places through contracts with HEIs and may support the student directly through bursaries. There is a presumption, but rarely any legal compulsion, that successful students will, in due course, work for the purchasing agent (often, at the time of writing an individual trust; further health service reforms are now trying to consolidate groups of purchasing trusts into consortia). Bursaries can also appear elsewhere, either publicly funded (as in government support for intending teachers of shortage subjects, or the armed forces sponsorship of engineers) or privately (as when companies sponsor students). In September 1997 the Secretary of State for Health announced steps to pay all tuition fees (and to supply bursaries) for all medical and dental students from year 5 of their courses, as well as to move all nursing, midwifery and PAMs courses across to the NHS (with access to bursaries). No announcement was made about the consequences of this significant shift for research funding channelled through the funding councils and assessed in the RAE (DoH, 1997).

The effect is significantly to complicate the pattern of stake-holder interests in course design, delivery and quality evaluation (see also chapter 11). For example figure 10.3 sets out in diagrammatic form the different 'interests' and their priorities as the medical professions other than doctors have come into the academy.

Figure 10.3   Health care in higher education: Stake-holders

'Stake-holder' requirements	
• SPONSORS	Value for Money (VFM) Flexibility in planning Service reputation
• STUDENTS	The HE experience Professional preparation and prospects
• PROVIDERS (a) 'educational' (b) 'professional'	 academic values disciplinary integrity professional values, including identity competence
• END-USERS	competence continuous improvement

Responding to Dearing

The prospects of mainstream full-time undergraduates contributing to fees (see chapter 12) is potentially a sharp shock for this somewhat Byzantine system. Dearing's proposals may seem brutal, but are probably the fairest option if his other principles are also to be realized here. Students will pay the flat rate for each full-time equivalent year of their courses. If this makes some courses more expensive, there is a presumption of greater personal return. In areas (principally the other public services) where the prospects for such premia are unlikely, the obligation is on the government departments making use of the graduates directly to support the institutions (through contracts) and students (through bursaries). In certain cases (such as teaching of subjects where there are currently significant shortages) government payment of fees could have a significant positive effect.

In addition to endorsing the continuation and enhancement of these honourable traditions Dearing seeks to nail down 'professional' roles and responsibilities within the academy as discussed in chapter 14.

11 Quality and Standards

During the 1980s and 1990s at least as much outrage has been generated within UK higher education institutions about the arrangements for institutional accountability and quality as about the funding crisis that, at the end of the day, led to Dearing. There is a huge paradox here, because the UK has (and arguably always has had) the most intensively scrutinized and hence 'standardized' approach to these matters in the world. What is more, this is an area in which the state has only recently taken a formal role in all but a small part.

The Quality Wars

Examining how these two effects (the institutional outrage and the state interest) came about, through a brief history of the 'quality wars', provides a cautionary tale about the internal and external image of the British higher education system.

Figure 11.1 shows some of the major landmarks in the story. As the nineteenth century system expanded, 'validating' or 'awarding' universities took responsibility for the standards of awards made by the new foundations, just as the post-Robbins universities were required to establish 'academic advisory' committees. Even more authoritative for the public sector was the role of the Council for National Academic Awards and its predecessor bodies. Meanwhile both systems of higher education have made use of a universal system of external examining, recently described by Harold Silver as a 'secret history' (Silver, 1996). Professional and statutory bodies have also played a role throughout, accrediting courses for professional recognition and practice, as have HMI (latterly OFSTED) in terms of teacher education courses on both sides of the binary line, and all courses in the former public sector up to the reforms of the early 1990s.

There is no doubt that in the past decade not only has confidence waned in the outcomes of these systems, but also institutions themselves have come to be more and more resentful. Overview analyses ascribe both features to a general move in public service and aspects of the private sector towards 'the audit society'. Certainly at the heart of the universities' problem is the question of public confidence to which they have collectively applied too little attention, too late.

Figure 11.1   Historical framework of external quality assurance

- validating and awarding universities
- professional and statutory bodies
- HMI and OFSTED
- external examiners
- post-Robbins 'academic advisory committees'
- CNAA (1961–1992)
- Academic Audit Unit (1989–1992)
- The watershed of the 1992 FHE — audit and assessment
- The QAA (1997)
- Dearing's mission for external examiners and QAA

The UGC sector picked up some signals of increasing public concern through the late 1980s and responded with such initiatives as the Jarratt Report on *Efficiency in Universities* (CVCP, 1985), and the Reynolds Report on *Academic Standards in Universities* (CVCP, 1986), which was accompanied by guidelines on external examining and established the short-lived Academic Audit Unit. Almost simultaneously a Committee of Enquiry chaired by Sir Norman Lindop looked into academic quality control on the other side of the binary line, and recommended a progressive movement of authority to the institutions themselves. The CNAA responded by setting up an hierarchy of relationships under their charter, the highest level of which was to be 'accreditation' (Lindop, 1985).

But the watershed, representing a new and much expanded role for the state in these processes, was again the 1992 Further and Higher Education Act. The Academic Audit Unit (AAU), which had been run by the CVCP, was swept into a sector-wide Higher Education Quality Council and the three new funding councils were statutorily required to have Quality Assessment Committees managing the 'assessment' of the work they funded on a subject-by-subject basis. A dual system of 'audit' of institutions' management of the quality assurance process and subject-based 'assessment' (both resulting in published reports), has been maintained from that point under almost relentless attack for its expense, intrusiveness, and claimed methodological weaknesses.

The government's intentions in setting out on this course were various. At one level they had simply to sort out and reassign previous functions and staff. At a higher philosophical and policy level the drive for increased, comparative public information about provision, independently verified, not only had a 'citizen's charter' feel to it; it also fitted a more general political mistrust of professionals and suppliers. Finally, they were keen to have teaching quality assessment informing funding decisions, as have the four successive rounds of research assessment since 1986. The English Funding Council has yet to take this step (beyond the creation of a Development Fund to spread good practice revealed in the assessments), although both the Scots and the Welsh have allocated additional places and funds in response. The contrast with research funding, where very substantial funds are now moved around the system, is extreme. Following the 1992 RAE exercise roughly half of the funds went to 12 institutions, while preliminary analysis of the consequences of the 1996 exercise suggest that, once some temporary moderating factors have worked their way through, the concentration will be even more extreme.

In one respect, however, the institutional campaign has borne fruit. The weak spot of the official processes was undoubtedly the duplication of effort and responsibility involved in the twin requirements of 'audit' and 'assessment', to which ministers responded by convening a Joint Planning Group (of the funding councils and the institutions' representative bodies) to design a unified system. In December 1996 this group produced what is essentially the blueprint for the new Quality Assurance Agency (QAA) (which came into being in April 1997), based on a cycle of subject or programme reviews (but still with a whole-institution overlay) incorporating tentative moves towards making institutions explicitly define the standards chosen for courses and their assessment (Joint Planning Group for Quality Assurance in Higher Education, 1996). As will be seen below, Dearing has considerably expanded intentions for the new agency.

From Quality to Standards

Almost simultaneously the HEQC brought out the final report of their Graduate Standards Programme (GSP), an extensive, multistranded investigation of institutional practice, problems and perspectives on the key issue of uniformity and national understanding of the standards implied by awards. As figure 11.2 indicates, most of their practical recommendations anticipate or converge with those of the Dearing Report.

This progressive shift in focus from attention to quality, especially the quality of the student experience, to confirmation of standards captures several developmental themes in the recent history of UK higher education. In one respect it represents a movement from the priority of competition between institutions, based particularly on 'league tables' derived from quality assessment to the restoration of collaboration, as in mutual assurance of threshold, output standards. In another it reflects a changed understanding of accountability, with simple market imperatives replaced by national standards. In these senses it is perhaps one of the decisive arenas for the Dearing Committee's vision of a fundamentally unified, if diverse sector.

Against this background it is salutary to list the perceptions (and in some cases) the reality of what has apparently gone wrong in the assurance of

Figure 11.2   Graduate Standards Programme: Recommendations

- Five actions to increase **clarity and explicitness** by:

    (i)   promoting and supporting institutional explicitness about standards;
    (ii)   agreeing to a range of dimensions against which the intended outcomes of degrees should be plotted;
    (iii) delineating a descriptive awards framework;
    (iv)   providing a typology of programmes and means of profiling their intended outcomes;
    (v)   agreeing a UK-wide system of student transcripts.

- Seven actions to increase **comparability and security and to strengthen academic judgment** by:

    (vi)   ensuring that intended standards are given close attention in the design and approval of programmes;
    (vii)   increasing the training and development opportunities for internal assessors and examiners;
    (viii) providing new fora in which examiners may review their practice and calibrate standards;
    (ix)   strengthening external examining;
    (x)   aligning assessment conventions and benchmarking practice;
    (xi)   developing the use of archives and other data to evaluate standards;
    (xii)   providing new opportunities for subject associations and PSBs to participate in the identification and review of standards.

- Two actions to progress work on **threshold standards** by:

    (xiii) ensuring that each institution clarifies its own threshold standards;
    (xiv)   preparing a project specification for the review of the current honours degree and classification system.

Source: HEQC, 1997.

standards and quality: declining public confidence in what constitutes a degree (or other HE qualification); uneasiness (in a minority of cases justified) about the entrepreneurial activity of institutions in using their degree-awarding powers through franchises and other examples of sub-contracted delivery; the weakness of subject and professional association links with the developing curriculum; and above all, the sheer weight of assessment now required of examiners, internal and external.

Responding to Dearing

Dearing is uncompromising about the questions of public confidence and collective responsibility raised by the quality and standards debate. For example, the Report envisages a role for the new single quality agency (the QAA) significantly stronger than that recommended by its progenitors, the funding councils and the institutions' representative bodies.

The key relevant recommendations are as follows:

We recommend that:

- *the Quality Assurance Agency should specify criteria for franchising arrangements;*

- *these criteria should rule out serial franchising, and include a normal presumption that the franchisee should have only one higher education partner;*

- *franchising partners should jointly review and, if necessary, amend existing arrangements to ensure that they meet the criteria, and should both certify to the Agency that arrangements conform with the criteria;*

- *there should be periodic checks by the Agency on the operation of franchise arrangements to verify compliance;*

- *after 2001, no franchising should take place either in the UK or abroad except where compliance with the criteria has been certified by the Quality Assurance Agency (recommendation 23).*

We recommend that the representative bodies and funding bodies amend the remit of the Quality Assurance Agency to include:

- *quality assurance and public information;*

- *standards verification;*

- *the maintenance of the qualifications framework;*

- *a requirement that the arrangements for these are encompassed in a code of practice which every institution should be required formally to adopt, by 2001/02, as a condition of public funding (recommendation 24).*

We recommend to the Quality Assurance Agency that its early work should include:

- *to work with institutions to establish small, expert teams to provide benchmark information on standards, in particular threshold standards, operating within the framework of qualifications, and completing the task by 2000;*

- *to work with universities and other degree-awarding institutions to create, within three years, a UK-wide pool of academic staff recognized by the Quality Assurance Agency, from which institutions must select external examiners;*

- *to develop a fair and robust system for complaints relating to educational provision;*

- *to review the arrangements in place for granting degree-awarding powers (recommendation 25).*

We recommend to the representative bodies and the funding bodies that the Board of the Quality Assurance Agency should, as soon as possible, include a student and an international member (recommendation 26).

We recommend to the government that it takes action, either by amending the powers of the Privy Council or by ensuring that conditions can be placed on the flow of public funds, to enable the removal of degree-awarding powers where the Quality Assurance Agency demonstrates that the power to award degrees has been seriously abused (recommendation 64).

This is a politically rich mixture of carrots and sticks. By returning to (and further developing) their historical commitment to collective assurance of standards (and we do not accept the conventional wisdom that it is simply growth that has made this apparently more difficult) the institutions have the prospects of reducing the amount of agency-based external scrutiny. Equally, in terms of the Dearing compact, it is crystal clear that the institutional comfort associated with more secure rates and processes of funding is in return for clarity about quality and standards to be delivered. Specific challenges include the coordination of resourcing of the network of external examiners (on which Dearing's assumption about a 60-day annual commitment is almost certainly unrealistic).

Part 4

Resources

12 Supporting Students

Those concerned about the demonstrable increase in student hardship as the higher education system expanded and the Conservative government 'reformed' its patterns of student finance have had to face some difficult issues: the relative generosity of the state package in international terms; its hugely regressive effect in terms of return to income groups; and the overall high personal rates of return to graduates in work. Nonetheless, along with the funding of institutions, this circle (of apparently generous yet inadequate public investment) was one of the major tasks of the Dearing Inquiry to square.

Before Robbins

The history leading up to this position is instructive. Government and university policy on grants and fees was almost exclusively concerned with full-time students until the post-Robbins expansion of higher education. Before the Second World War financial support for students was very limited, with many students, especially at Oxford and Cambridge, relying on private, family financial support. There was a small number of state scholarships, around 360 a year, and a small number of LEA awards with a 'boarding' element. Such awards were based on achievement at Higher School Certificate level, and the award of a university place, and sometimes of an exhibition or scholarship. Such university *ad hoc* financing, from endowments, special funds and the like, exacerbated the piecemeal nature of a national system wherein different LEAs adopted widely varying practices for awarding grants. Most LEA awards covered fees but only a small proportion of maintenance costs, and many adopted a system of part grant, part loan — repayable once the graduate was in employment.

The number of full-time students in universities was just over 50,000 in 1938–39, and this fell for obvious reasons during the War to 35,648 in 1943–44, and rose again to only 37,839 in 1944–45. However, the War also saw the first significant move towards the later universal system of financial support for full-time students. The government was concerned that 'the numbers studying engineering, chemistry and physics showed some signs of dropping during the second year of the War' (Gosden, 1976, p. 148). Radio and technical expertise were needed urgently for the War effort and the government therefore instituted a system of two-year bursaries, through the Winless Personnel Committee, to support students in relevant subject areas. 'The aim was entirely materialist and immediate, to meet the pressure for trained personnel for radio work, and some forms of engineering and chemistry' (ibid.).

In 1943 the Norwood Committee reported and advocated the ending of the existing School Certificate and Higher School Certificate system. It laid the foundations, in effect, for the tripartite secondary educational system which characterized UK education until the Crosland reforms of the mid-1960s. Pressure from the rapid growth of the 'sixth-form sector' in secondary education resulting from these new structures of the 1950s and 1960s, became the primary underlying cause of the eventual expansion of the university system from the mid-1960s onwards. (There were of course socioeconomic factors which, in the wider context, underlay this general expansion of 16–19 education and higher education in the mid-twentieth century. These are discussed in chapter 2.)

As is the way with such changes, however, there was a considerable time-lag between the developments of an administration and the necessary creation of a universal and equitable student funding system. Although Harold Laski had correctly written in 1943 that the two world wars had led 'to the certainty of a planned society' (Laski in Gosden, 1976, p. 425), a planned and coherent HE system did not emerge until the 1960s and the framework created by the Robbins Report and the Crosland reforms.

As far as student funding structures were concerned the situation remained incoherent and unplanned through the 1940s and 1950s as the university system began to expand. In 1946 the government introduced supplementary awards which enabled most students who had gained entrance scholarships to university to have the value of their awards brought up to the level of state scholarships, meeting both fees and maintenance costs. The Ministry of Education also exerted pressure upon LEAs to ensure that proper provision was made for those who gained awards. 'By 1951 about four-fifths of (students') awards were calculated on a full maintenance basis. By the end of the decade virtually all . . . awards were on this basis' (Gosden, 1983, p. 144). However, many students still received part of their financing as a loan rather than a grant.

Student numbers increased steadily through the 1940s and 1950s: in 1946–47 there were 68,456 full-time students in universities; by 1958–59 this had risen to over 100,000; and by 1964–65 to over 138,000. The predominant pattern of student life was also changing. At most universities, until the 1950s, most undergraduates lived at home and travelled daily to their local university. At Leeds, for example, in 1938–39, 56.5 per cent of undergraduates lived at home. But, by 1950–51, this had fallen to 41.4 per cent and fell much further of course through subsequent years.

These evolutionary changes were codified and a properly planned system of student finance brought into being from 1960, through a committee chaired by Colin Anderson. The Anderson Committee recommended, and the government agreed, that any student with a minimum of two 'A' Levels who had been accepted for entrance to a university should be entitled to a mandatory award to cover not only fees but maintenance costs. The government also decided that these awards should be made on a uniform basis through the LEAs. All these provisions were included in the Education Act of 1962.

It was in this climate of expansion 'and of growing realization that both higher education needed to be planned and that the State had an increasing stake-holding in the finance and policy development of universities' that the Robbins Committee was established in 1961 to review the development of higher education. The rising pressure on university places, a result largely of the expansion of secondary and particularly grammar school education post-16, was a key consideration for the Robbins Committee. The figures, cited by Gosden, were quite dramatic. In 1955 there had been 70,000 applications for university places and 18,000 admissions: by 1960 the figures had risen respectively to 151,000 and 22,650, and by 1961 to 190,000 and 25,000. The universal availability of relatively generous student finance, and the opportunity for bright middle-class and lower-middle-class adolescents to spend three years away at university, were obviously key elements in this rapid expansion of demand.

This is not the context in which to discuss the far-reaching consequences of the Robbins Report overall. Relevant here is the combination of rapid growth and expansion of full-time student numbers and the universal system of mandatory awards for fees and maintenance, the latter importantly being subject to parental means-testing. As indicated in chapter 1, by the early 1980s student numbers in universities had grown to 800,000, the very large majority of whom were middle-class, 18–21-years-old, full-time and studying and living at a university away from home. Virtually all students were in receipt of a grant, though, for those from more affluent backgrounds, the means-testing element meant that parents were expected to contribute the large bulk of maintenance costs.

The politics of this issue were (and remain) passionate and intense. Like mortgage interest tax relief, free tuition in higher education has been regarded for decades as an 'untouchable' middle-class benefit, especially for those parents who have invested heavily in private secondary school education in order to position their children to benefit. George Walden, one of a series of Conservative junior ministers responsible for higher education who have subsequently sought to distance themselves from the policies pursued by their Secretaries of State (see also the references to Eric Forth and Nigel Forman below) tells a story of challenging the late John Smith, Leader of the Opposition, about the irrationality of both and the need to speak out. 'I will if she will' was the reply (Walden, 1996, p. 174).

Full-time Students, Fees and Maintenance

Robbins had little to say about the pattern of full-time student support and hence inadvertently opened the hairpin of committed expenditure further dramatically widened by the Baker reforms. As a consequence, through grants, fees and access to the benefit system the UK began the 1980s (1979 was always regarded as the baseline from which campaigners attempted to restore full-time student entitlement) with the most generous system of support in the OECD group, with a special premium for the majority who (unlike their counterparts in the rest of Europe) lived away from home. Thus middle-class families, many of whom had effectively 'purchased' an advantage in university entrance by opting out of the State system and sending their children to private schools, gathered a huge bargain (Adonis, 1997). The investigation of the 'social wage' carried out by Tom Sefton (STICERD) and summarized in figure 12.1 demonstrates this effect.

The Conservative government initially tried to tackle this issue by charging fees (as described in chapter 1), but subsequently alighted on a policy of reducing access to benefit, capping the total maintenance entitlement, and progressively (from 1990) redefining a proportion of the latter as loans (the final target for this proportion was set as 50 per cent). Simultaneously 'access funds' (in reality 'hardship funds') were provided to institutions to deal with individual cases (full-time students only, and then only given evidence that they had taken up their loan entitlement). A new agency — the Student Loans Company — was established, had a rocky initial ride, but has now recovered sufficiently to be considered by Dearing a suitable shell for the envisaged 'Student Support Agency'.

As a result of these changes there have been a number of studies of the effects on the financial circumstances of full-time students (see, for example, Callender and Kempson, 1996; Winn and Stevenson, 1997). Many of these suffer from the distortions of averaging and reversion to the mean; there are clearly many middle-class families for whom publicly supported higher education remains a significant bargain, just as there are many students from poorer families facing the prospects of crippling public and private debt. Figure 12.2 provides three snapshots in time of the overall changes in the pattern of student income between 1988 and 1996.

Supporting Part-timers

Moreover, in tune with the emphasis on lifetime learning, Dearing also had to deal with the circumstances of the majority of students in the system who are now not on full-time first degree courses studying away from home.

Until the 1980s there was little discussion of how, if at all, part-time students should be financed and supported for their university studies. There were exceptions: from early in the twentieth century the DES Responsible Body (RB) system had provided earmarked funding for the support of extra-mural provision in the majority of the existing universities. By the 1970s such funding normally accounted for around a half of the total costs of most such Extra-mural or Continuing Education Departments. The RB grant was made in respect of liberal adult education teaching post costs, and was calculated on a partly historical, partly student numbers basis. In addition, the regional responsibility for such provision was taken into account. The contribution from adult students themselves through class fees was a relatively small proportion of total revenue.

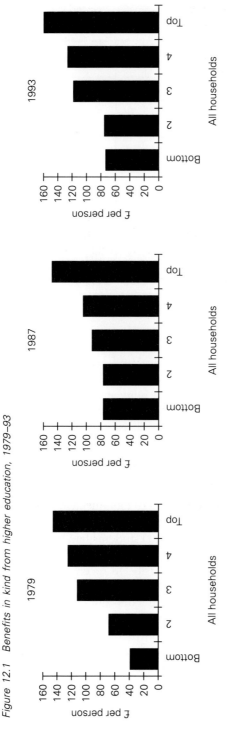

Figure 12.1 Benefits in kind from higher education, 1979–93

Note: The charts show that the distribution of benefits in kind from HE distinctly is 'pro-rich'. The shape of the distribution does not change significantly over the period 1979 to 1993.
Source: Sefton, 1997.

Figure 12.2   Source of student income, 1988/89, 1992/93 and 1995/96 (students aged under 26 only)

Source of income	1998/89 (£)	1998/89 (%)	1992/93 (£)	1992/93 (%)	1995/96 (£)	1995/96 (%)
Grant	1159	38	1300	38	1063	23
Parental contribution	955	32	902	26	1002	22
Student loan	—	—	291	8	628	14
Earnings	187	6	237	7	621	14
Gifts	268	9	235	7	494	11
Loans	108	4	146	4	278	6
Withdrawn savings	124	4	80	2	284	6
Other	230	8	269	8	205	4
Total income	**3031**	**100**	**3464**	**100**	**4575**	**100**

Source: Callender and Kempson, 1996.

The bulk of the balance of the costs came through central university funds for the costs of the administrative, clerical and managerial staff, and for a proportion of the costs of the lecturing staff. In addition, of course, the university met the semi-hidden costs of buildings, heating and lighting and the like. This system continued, with major review, restructuring and reduction, through the 1980s until, with the ending of the binary division and the creation of the funding councils, the large bulk of continuing education in the traditional universities was accredited and 'mainstreamed' in the mid-1990s.

The second major exception came with the creation of the Open University in 1966 by Harold Wilson and Jennie Lee. Open University students' fees formed only a relatively small proportion of the Open University's overall income, with the bulk coming through direct grant, originally from the DES rather than the UGC. By 1981, approximately 150,000 students had been admitted to the Open University, 45,000 had graduated, 45,000 had left without graduating and 60,000 were still registered with the University. In recent years, with the squeeze on university funding, student fees have risen markedly.

With the exception of part-time extra-mural students, where as indicated earlier separate financial arrangements were in place, universities have until recently paid little attention to adult or part-time undergraduate students. A small proportion of mature students was admitted to full-time undergraduate degree programmes and such students were eligible for a slightly enhanced grant, depending upon their circumstances (family responsibilities etc.). However, with the creation of the polytechnics, a much more heterogeneous student body came into being. Many students were locally based, living at home, and over

21; many of these were also part-time and either supporting themselves financially or being supported by their employers to undertake vocationally oriented programmes.

The argument for equity, in terms of funding, between part-time and full-time students was pursued with vigour by the CE community in the 1980s, but to little effect. The pragmatic response from the DES and others was always that this would cost a significant additional amount, that demand for part-time programmes on the present financial basis was buoyant and expanding, and that there was little pressure from HEIs, the CVCP et al. for change.

However, by the 1990s two factors in particular had made this stance untenable. The proportion of mature and part-time students within the greatly expanded system had risen sharply. No longer could part-time, mature students be regarded as a minor 'add-on' to the mainstream system. Secondly, the rapid adoption by the large majority of HEIs of credit-based modular systems meant that the distinctions between part-time and full-time students became at least theoretically redundant (see chapter 7). Only the persisting and increasingly artificial differences in the funding regime prolonged the distinction. The announcement by HEFCE in late 1996 (*Circular 21/96*) that, from 1998–99, the funding for teaching would be based on a volume measure irrespective of whether students were full or part-time, holds out the prospect of bringing this long-running anomaly to an end.

Squaring the Circle

The second half of the Main Report of the Dearing Committee is dominated by the issue of student support and graduate contributions to the costs of their higher education. A sequence of chapters identifies the current and projected funding gap (17), an exploration of the question of responsibility for supporting higher education, concluding firmly that the beneficiaries (including graduates) should bear part of the costs (18), the implications for funding institutions (19 — see also chapter 13 below), an analysis of the options available (20), and the outline of a programme for assessing and collecting contributions (21). Throughout, the Committee carefully balances the key variables: the relationship between state support for maintenance and the costs to individuals; the scope for means-testing state support; the availability of state-supported loans and their repayment terms; and the range of transactions required between the students, the institution and the state agencies concerned. A sophisticated model was also constructed for the Committee to evaluate the potential outcome of different options and is described in the technical reports (NCIHE, 1997, Reports 12 and 14).

From this array the Committee tests two versions of a graduate tax and rejects them, largely on political grounds, before setting out four core options and comparing them with the present system of grants and loans. These are set out below in summary form.

Figure 12.3   Dearing: Graduate contribution options

	Living costs support	Tuition contribution
• **Existing system**	50% means tested grant 50% loan	None
• **Option A: Maintenance contribution**	100% income contingent loan	None
• **Option B: Tuition contribution**	50% means tested grant 50% income contingent loan	25% contribution with income contingent loan
• **Option C: Means tested tuition contribution**	100% income contingent loan	25% means tested contribution with no loan
• **Option D: Tuition contribution with restoration of maintenance grants**	100% means tested grant	25% contribution with income contingent loan

Source: NCIHE, 1997, Summary Report, Table 3.

Steering a careful path between the policy requirements of maintaining (and ideally enhancing) access and equity, and the strict economic prohibition of no more government money, the Committee opted for variant B as the best solution in the circumstances.

In responding to the Dearing Report in July 1997 the government clearly acted courageously in accepting up-front the principle of graduate contributions. They then proceeded to outline a scheme which is apparently built on not one of the Dearing options and runs the danger of falling into several of the traps that the Committee was anxious to avoid (DfEE, 1997). Briefly, the official scheme would convert all maintenance grants into loans, adapt but means-test the fee element, calibrate the whole entitlement so that no family would pay more than under the present arrangements, and offer a special 'extra' loan of £250 to students meeting so far unspecified conditions of hardship. Commentators — not least the institutions — have pointed out how this package would result in students from poorer families owing more than those better off when in work, how the transaction costs of a means-tested fee would be likely to absorb a very considerable element of the notional £1000 per head, and how the net effect of advancing more money in loans would be dramatically to increase public expenditure in the years in which the loans are advanced without any direct benefit to the colleges and universities.

This last problem exposes a further anomaly, also commented on in the Report on the basis of international evidence. Current rules for government accounting include the full value of loans as if they were grants (with no prospect of repayment) in the year in which they are advanced. Following international practice, and without violating the criteria established at Maastricht for public expenditure restrictions, it should be possible for only the implied subsidy (favourable interest rates and a provision for non-repayment) to be accounted for in this way (NCIHE, 1997, Main Report 20.87–88).

Whatever the outcome for full-time students, Dearing's recommendations for part-timers are less comprehensive and effectively piecemeal. They include a combination of possibly restored benefits, 'forgiven' fees (for which institutions should be reimbursed) for certain categories of students (such as the unemployed), and eligibility for institutionally-administered access funds. The simple extension, on a *pro rata* basis of full-time entitlements, urged by many submissions to the Committee (especially those which, like UACE's, came from a special perspective on lifelong learning), is rejected, partly on the grounds of cost, partly because a Committee survey of part-time students showed a significant proportion (35 per cent of those in work) having fees paid by employers (although the accuracy of this data has been questioned (Ward, 1997)). In several contexts the Dearing Committee has been criticized for not requiring more of employers; here they were anxious not to let an employer liability (if only moral) slip across to the State (ibid., Main Report 20.6–12).

Student Unions

Among the most vociferous groups in opposition to student fees as the Committee was working was the National Union of Students (NUS). Paradoxically this powerful force (now well represented by former presidents in the Labour Parliamentary Lobby) had moved to accept the principle of loans for maintenance grants, despite its hugely regressive effect, as set out above.

The Dearing Committee included a Student Union Officer, one might imagine at the insistence of the Opposition at the time of its formation. Much was also made of the NUS move to accept that restoration of grants and benefits to their 1979 levels was an unattainable goal, and the Union's acceptance that some further contribution from students as eventual beneficiaries from higher education was inevitable. Regressive though such a stance might be, the NUS remains implacably opposed to any direct levy of fees.

On the student role in governance and the internal running of institutions, the Dearing Report has, however, come down very positively on the side of formal participation. There are no echoes of the 1994 Act with its attempt (perhaps leading to the resignation of another junior minister, Nigel Forman, whose heart never seemed to be in tune with Conservative back-benchers baying for this particular sacrifice) to circumscribe official Union activities.

The Committee's Report has been widely recognized as 'student-centred', with a special emphasis on students as consumers and clients of higher education as well as 'members' of institutions. There are, of course, other dimensions to the higher education experience as captured by the following institutional submission:

We trust . . . that the Committee will recognize in its report the critical importance to the success of UK higher education of ensuring that all students have a secure, well-supported and caring environment within which to pursue their studies. It is not fashionable to argue that students have a right to enjoy their higher education; we urge the Committee not to be afraid of the unfashionable . . . (ibid., Report 1, 5.1)

Responding to Dearing

Dearing bites the bullet on student contributions, with a range of options that incorporate income-contingent contributions by graduates in work to the costs of their higher education (maintenance and a flat-rate fee) as advanced to them by the state. The Report also takes some steps towards restoration of lost benefits and more equitable treatment of part-timers, but stops short of the full agnosticism as to mode recommended by organizations like UACE. Finally, he makes a number of suggestions to tidy up the enormous complexity (and costs) of the official transactions that are associated with administering the system.

The key relevant recommendations are as follows:

We recommend to the government that:

- *it considers the possibility of restoring to full-time students some entitlement to social security benefits, as part of its forthcoming review of the social security system. This review should include consideration of two particular groups in current difficulty, those who temporarily withdraw from higher education due to illness and those with dependent children aged over 16;*

- *the total available to institutions for Access Funds should be doubled with effect from 1998/99 and that the scope of the funds should be extended to facilitate participation by students who would otherwise be unable to enter higher education (recommendation 5).*

We recommend:

- *to the funding bodies that they provide funding for institutions to provide learning support for students with disabilities;*

- *to the Institute for Learning and Teaching in Higher Education (see Recommendation 14) that it includes the learning needs of students with disabilities in its research, programme accreditation and advisory activities;*

- *to the government that it extends the scope of the Disabled Students Allowance so that it is available without a parental means-test and to part-time students, postgraduate students and those who have become disabled who wish to obtain a second higher education qualification (recommendation 6).*

We recommend to students' unions and institutions that they review, on a regular basis, the services offered to their students and adapt them as necessary, in particular to meet the needs of part-time students (recommendation 12).

We recommend to the government that it reviews annually the total level of support for student living costs taking into account the movement of both prices and earnings (recommendation 70).

We recommend to the government that:

- *from 1998/99 it should enable institutions to waive tuition fees for part-time students in receipt of Jobseeker's Allowance or certain family benefits;*

- *as part of its forthcoming review of the social security system, it should review the interaction between entitlement to benefits and part-time study, with a view to ensuring that there are no financial disincentives to part-time study by the unemployed or those on low incomes;*

- *it should extend eligibility for Access Fund payments to part-time students from 1998/99, and additional funding should be made available for this purpose (recommendation 76).*

We recommend to the government that, once the interim bursary scheme expires, it establishes permanent arrangements for the equitable support of students of dance, drama and stage management at institutions which are not in receipt of public funds (recommendation 77).

We recommend to the government that it introduces, by 1998/99, income contingent terms for the payment of any contribution towards living costs or tuition costs sought from graduates in work (recommendation 78).

On a balance of considerations, we recommend to the government that it introduces arrangements for graduates in work to make a flat rate contribution of around 25 per cent of the average cost of higher education tuition, through an income contingent mechanism, and that it ensures that the proportion of tuition costs to be met by the contribution cannot be increased without an independent review and an affirmative resolution of both Houses of Parliament. The contributions made by graduates in work in this way should be reserved for meeting the needs of higher education (recommendation 79).

We recommend to the government that it looks urgently at alternative and internationally accepted approaches to national accounting which do not treat the repayable part of loans in the same way as grants to students (recommendation 80).

We recommend to the government that the Inland Revenue should be used as the principal route for the collection of income contingent contributions from graduates in work, on behalf of the Student Loans Company (recommendation 82).

We recommend to the government that it establishes, as soon as possible, a unified Student Support Agency with responsibility for:

- *assessing the eligibility of individuals for various kinds of public support;*

- *administering graduate contributions on an income contingent basis;*

- *means-testing and paying grants for students' living costs;*

- *making per capita tuition payments to institutions according to the number of students they enrol (recommendation 83).*

At the time of writing the possible outcomes of the student support debate are very delicately poised, with the government having made a commitment to seeking a contribution to fees from students in work (and to converting all maintenance support into loans) but without clear commitments to other parts of the so-called compact (see chapter 20 below). Dearing's careful balance of the variables is clearly fragile, while there is also disappointment about some of the roads not taken on support for part-timers. Meanwhile, more radical, overarching solutions such as Individual Learning Accounts (ILAs) — although investigated by Dearing (ibid., report 13) — have been put on hold.

13　Supporting Institutions

Future historians will agree that it was the funding crisis facing institutions in 1996–97, and the threat by a majority of vice-chancellors to take the law into their own hands which precipitated the establishment of the Dearing Committee. Members of the CVCP are, however, increasingly aware that they are unlikely to achieve comfort on the funding question without concessions and fulfilment of obligations on other fronts such as accountability and governance.

Funding

The headline issue for institutions during the past 15 years has been under-funded expansion. Figure 13.1, on the unit of resource from public funds available to universities and colleges, shows a drop of approximately 40 per cent overall, although the resetting of the index in 1989 (following the formation of the PCFC) disguises some significant discontinuities, especially during the 1980s as the traditional universities held up their unit of resource by absorbing cuts and the PCFC sector expanded rapidly at marginal costs (essentially by taking on students for the local authority fee only).

From the perspective of central government the proportion of GDP and GNP dedicated to higher education has remained almost constant, and if anything risen slightly in recent years, as set out in figure 13.2.

What is more, the government can also apparently point to a fairly respectable (mid-range) performance for public investment when compared with the usual OECD comparator countries (See figure 13.3).

This is where the full force of under-funded expansion kicks in. Crudely, as numbers have grown and because of the apparently uncapped entitlement to maintenance and fees support unleashed by the Baker–Clarke expansion, the proportion of public investment going to students rather than to institutions has increased disproportionately (See figure 13.4). This is the margin that Dearing was invited to tap by considering student contributions. The current government clearly anticipated that he would do so by addressing maintenance only. In fact for reasons set out in the last chapter, he opted to invade the fees band as well.

Of the funds which do flow directly to universities (block grant and local authority fee) it is difficult, but important, to try to identify what they are for. Prior to the 1992 Act the UGC/UFC carried an approximately 40 per cent premium per student supposedly to cover the costs of research (with increasing

Figure 13.1   Unit public funding, 1979–97

Year	University	HEFCE	Polytechnic
	INDEX		
1979/80	100		100
1980/81	106		99
1981/82	103		94
1982/83	106		89
1983/84	107		82
1984/85	106		79
1985/86	103		78
1986/87	102		79
1987/88	105		76
1988/89	103		75
1989/90	100		—
1990/91		100	
1991/92		93	
1992/93		87	
1993/94		83	
1994/95		81	
1995/96		79	
1996/97		76	

Sources: CVCP, 1995b; DfEE, 1996.

discomfort about the level of audit and accountability). PCFC funding (follow-ing the Roith Report) was limited to a token amount, all directed towards particular projects (Committee of Enquiry on Research in the Polytechnics and Colleges Sector, 1990). Following the 1992 reforms, and access by the former PCFC sector to the Research Assessment Exercise, research funding was explic-itly separated and audited, made available to new universities and colleges on a competitive (mostly quality-related basis, although in recognition of the low base from which they started strongly performing new entrants were given access to a small stream of earmarked 'development' funding, which they have retained under slightly different rules after the 1996 exercise). Briefly, research

Figure 13.2   Public expenditure on higher education in the UK as a percentage of GDP, 1976–95

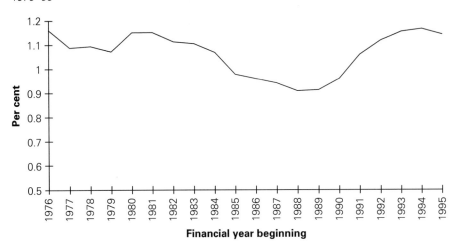

Financial year beginning

Source: NCIHE, 1997, Main Report, Chart 3.15.

funding was also relatively protected from the 'efficiency gains' prescribed by successive spending rounds, although that advantage has now been removed.

As figure 13.5 indicates, however, funding council funds for research are significantly concentrated, and although divisions of the league may be emerging, a gulf remains between old and new.

One interesting inference may be drawn from this story: before the late-1990s drive to account more precisely for expenditure traditional institutions were probably using a proportion of their research funds to support teaching (the outcomes of HEFCE teaching quality assessments seem to confirm this, especially when overall institutional 'prosperity' is analysed as a variable [HEFCE, 1995a]); similarly, given their flying start, many PCFC institutions must have been using teaching funding to support research before 1992.

The concentration on dispersal of research monies from the funding councils was probably the issue on which the Dearing Committee was most intensely lobbied during its working life, especially from those institutions wishing to see the creation of a research super-league including only themselves (Broers et al., 1996). Tension was increased by the concurrent outcomes of the 1996 Research Assessment Exercise.

The Dearing Committee attempted to take a more holistic view and to separate out present and potential funding streams according to their intended purposes. These included a preservation (with reform) of the so-called 'dual funding' scheme. Research councils would be responsible for fully funding projects and programmes on a prospective basis (formally, after the last transfer across the boundary they are already obliged to do so, but clearly do not — often as a result of collusive negotiation with research teams to achieve more projects with the same quantum of funds). Simultaneously the retrospective

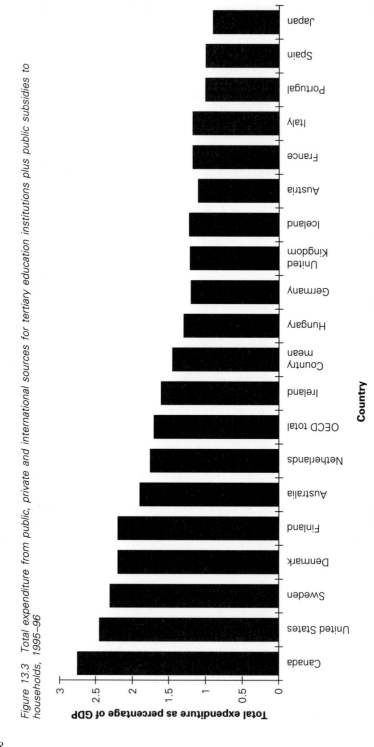

Figure 13.3 Total expenditure from public, private and international sources for tertiary education institutions plus public subsidies to households, 1995–96

Source: NCIHE, 1997, Chart 3.17.

Figure 13.4 Public expenditure on higher education in the UK (1995–96 prices)

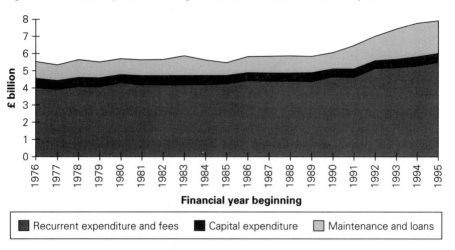

Note: Includes recurrent and capital grants to institutions, publicly funded tuition fees, funding from research councils, expenditure on student maintenance grants and net expenditure on student loans.
Source: NCIHE, 1997, Main Report, Chart 3.14.

analysis of research quality through the RAE would continue, and enable institutions to set their own developmental agenda, with one important proviso: a cut-off point (at the current level 3(a), implying at least some research of international significance) and two incentives to institutions only to enter if they are confident of reaching this level. The positive incentive would be the identification of a *per capita*-based stream of funding to support all teachers in higher education (also in line with the Committee's thinking on the distinctive role of the research environment in higher education, as discussed in chapter 8). The negative incentive would be the loss of these funds for unsuccessful departments which did not reach the 'safety-net' level of current 3(b). The two final streams include coordination of R and D support offered by other government departments (especially the DTI and the Department of Health) with the strategies of regional agencies (as discussed in chapter 15 below) and a special initiative (personally fronted by Sir Ron) to establish from government and industrial sources a loan fund for significant scientific investment (NCIHE, 1997, Main Report Chapter 11).

Two other scene-setting variables are important. Before incorporation in 1988, polytechnics and colleges formally held no assets from one year to the next; any reserves or surpluses were at the grace and favour of their managing local authorities. Similarly, they had no direct responsibility for maintenance and development of the physical estate and except under peculiar conditions (including those which pertained in some of the London polytechnics as companies limited by guarantee) were unable or unlikely to attract substantial endowments or bequests. The role of capital funding was thus critical. UGC

Figure 13.5   HEFCE research funding as a percentage of T and R funding 1996–97

HEFCE research funding as a percentage of T and R funding		Institution
0.01–0.12	2	Luton, Central England
1.35–1.60	3	Lincolnshire and Humberside, Anglia Polytechnic, Thames Valley
2.32–6.63	25	Bournemouth, London Guildhall, Central Lancashire, Wolverhampton, Derby, Leeds Metropolitan, Teesside, Nottingham Trent, Liverpool John Moores, North London, Staffordshire, Greenwich, Huddersfield, West of England, Open, East London, Kingston, South Bank, Hertfordshire, De Montfort, Westminster, Northumbria, Sunderland, Manchester Metropolitan, Sheffield Hallam
7.70–8.86	3	Middlesex, Coventry, Plymouth
10.04–10.46	3	Brighton, Portsmouth, Oxford Brookes
18.64–20.23	3	Brunel, Goldsmiths, Salford
23.41–27.46	7	Aston, Cranfield, Bradford, Hull, Birkbeck, Royal Holloway, Kent
29.45–35.55	15	Keele, City, Loughborough, Durham, Liverpool, Queen Mary and Westfield, Leicester, Exeter, Leeds, Sheffield, Newcastle upon Tyne, Essex, Lancaster, Surrey, Bristol
36.99–39.25	10	Nottingham, Birmingham, Sussex, York, Bath, Southampton, Reading, Manchester, London, East Anglia
42.23–43.57	3	UMIST, Warwick, King's College
48.42–55.01	5	University College London, Imperial, Cambridge, Oxford, LSE
75.41	1	London Business School

Note: 'Groups' have been identified separated by at least one percentage point.
Source: Data from HEFCE, 1996c.

institutions before 1988 relied on a kind of DES roundabout for major capital projects, waiting their turn, for example, for new libraries. Public sector institutions negotiated intensively within local authorities over the latters' capital budgets.

It is no accident that the condition of the collective estate was an early source of anxiety for both the UFC and the PCFC, each of which commissioned large-scale surveys showing huge shortfalls in maintenance and investment (see HEFCE, 1993). Similar such problems have been revealed in terms of scientific and technical equipment, with the latest survey suggesting a funding gap of over £400million (NAPAG, 1996; PREST et al., 1996, 1997). Since 1992, and more especially since 1996, when the funding councils ceased separating a capital and a revenue stream in the grant and withdrew from supporting major capital projects on anything but a meagre matching basis, the problem of the estate has been pitched back firmly into the lap of the governing body of each institution.

The Conservative government, in its last two years, held out high hopes for the Private Finance Initiative (PFI) to bridge the gap in line with its strong ideological commitment to privatization. This was the basis for swingeing cuts in capital grant in 1995–96 and 1996–97. The Dearing Report confirms how illusory this proposition in fact was. Not only do PFI projects simply transfer liabilities onto (often more costly) revenue payments, but there is no willing queue of private sector investors lining up to share the risk with institutions on replacing routine scientific equipment or rotting window frames (NCIHE, 1997, Main Report 19.55).

John Bevan of the National Advisory Body used to refer to the theory of the 'impending precipice' when talking about the resource squeeze in higher education: the next cut will always be the fatal one, until it comes (and then somehow everyone adapts). But at what price do they adapt? It is remarkable how the managements of universities (traditional and new) and colleges succeeded relatively uniformly in keeping going in the face of the ratchet outlined above. Fundamentally the sector as a whole, as revealed in the funding councils' publications of aggregated financial performance and forecasts, have managed their recurrent margins down to almost nothing. It was the aggregate 1995 forecasts, indicating a majority of institutions about to tip into deficit and into non-compliance with the Financial Memorandum with the HEFCE that arguably prompted the CVCP 'top-up' fee rebellion, and eventually the Dearing Inquiry (HEFCE, 1995c).

While the Inquiry has gone on the position has deteriorated further. The HEFCE analysis of 1996 financial forecasts confirms a pattern of deficits from 1996–97 onwards with an increasing number of institutions below the line: 26 in 1994–95; 48 in 1995–96; and over 70 by 1999–2000. Simultaneously the proportion of reserves held as cash (as opposed to property) declines sharply over the period (22–16 per cent), as does capital expenditure (despite the difficulties alluded to above it will go down by 60 per cent between 1995 and 2000) (HEFCE, 1996a). This gloomy picture is compounded by a parallel analysis of Strategic Plans, with projected staff losses of 2600 by 2000 (1.3 per cent) and a drop in provision for building maintenance of over a quarter (HEFCE, 1996e).

Governance

For many constituencies, including lay interests outside the university and staff and student interests within it, responsibility for sorting out these problems lies with the proper authorities of governance (Boards and Councils) and management (vice-chancellors and their senior teams).

Formally, it is governance arrangements that constitute the most endur-ing legacy of the former binary divide. The traditional universities nearly all have individual royal charters, with quirks and characteristics reflecting live concerns at the time of their foundation. The new universities are almost all higher education corporations (some of the former London polytechnics are companies limited by guarantee) with degree-awarding powers vested in the corporation by statute (the 1992 Further and Higher Education Act). The com-position of supreme or governing bodies reflect these differences: Councils (and occasionally Courts) in the former case; the Board of Governors (operat-ing under an almost uniform set of Instruments and Articles of government approved by the Privy Council) in the latter.

This difference has led to a rather simplistic view of competing cultures: the 'academic democracy' of the chartered university, apparently guaranteed by the significant number of staff and student members on the Council, *versus* the 'managerialism' of the corporation, with its small but heavily influential group of 'independent' members (who are required to be in the majority) backing a determined executive (the vice-chancellor is normally the sole executive dir-ector) and a line management structure inherited from the local authority era.

In the most effective examples of each kind of institution it is not at all like this, of course. Traditional universities have never managed to sustain the practice of governance by eventual and universal consensus and remain effect-ive, while former polytechnic directorates without significant respect for aca-demic discourse and priorities have nearly always received their come-uppance (often at the cost of damaging institutional disruption). But there are some ironies. The typical traditional university Council, with its benches of local authority re-presentatives, of staff and student unions, and co-opted local dignitaries resembles nothing so much as some of the unwieldly former polytechnic governing bodies whose collective failure to overcome internal differences and bureaucratic inertia provided the most powerful stimulus to incorporation in 1988.

As hinted at above, it is common for lay interests and for politicians to declare that university governance has failed. There have indeed been occa-sional scandals (usually *ad hominem*) and a small number of financial crises, but overall this is an argument hard to sustain. The Nolan Committee, for example, gave governing bodies a generally good bill of health, while routine Funding Council audits of governance arrangements have found very little to complain about (Committee on Standards in Public Life, 1996).

In adjudicating between these alternative models Dearing appears to favour the new model over the old, especially on size. But his Report is also clear about the roles and responsibilities of staff and student governors — seeing them not as 'representatives' but as governors in their own right, and not liable to exclu-sion from any substantive business conducted by the Council or the Board. He is also tough on two further features which have provided points of contention over the past few years: the need for secure, transparent and above all speedy responses to complaints; and the conditions and responsibilities of sound aca-demic governance.

On this latter point Senates (in the traditional universities) and Academic Boards (in the new) share a common set of obligations: to underwrite all academic awards made in the institution's name. Dearing shows how and why this has occasionally slipped, especially as colleges and universities have taken short-cuts in the interests of income generation and interinstitutional competition (NCIHE, 1997, Main Report, Chapter 15).

Responding to Dearing

Dearing has attempted to tackle the funding of institutions in a number of coordinated ways:

1 through the exploration of further efficiency gains, including those which arise from the successful use of communications and information technology:
2 through careful separation of the different funding streams associated with research;
3 through independent review of staff pay and conditions (see also chapter 14);
4 through the encouragement of improved management systems and more sophisticated 'benchmarking';
5 through greater clarity in the roles and responsibilities of governing bodies, including to set and review performance targets;
6 through increased public investment, in line with the growth in GDP, on the assumption of a longer planning period (three years rather than one), and on the basis that funding councils and others (including an industrially supported capital grant scheme) are prepared to support sound collaborative schemes up-front;
7 through a qualified endorsement of the 'market principle', in responding to student demand;
8 through clearer national and sub-national arrangements for funding of both further and higher education (see also chapter 16 below); and
9 through the contributions of 'graduates in work' discussed in chapter 12.

The key relevant recommendations are as follows:

We recommend that the funding bodies, through the Joint Information Systems Committee (JISC), should continue to manage and fund, on a permanent basis, quality and cost-effective communications and information technology (C and IT) services for researchers and should, in due course, introduce charges for services on a volume-of-usage basis (recommendation 27).

We recommend to the funding bodies that the Joint Information Systems Committee (JISC) should be invited to report, within a year, on options to provide sufficient protected international bandwidth to support UK research (recommendation 28).

We recommend to the government that a new Arts and Humanities Research Council (AHRC) should be established as soon as possible (recommendation 29).

We recommend:

- *to the government that, with immediate effect, projects and programmes funded by the research councils meet their full indirect costs and the costs of premises and central computing, preferably through the provision of additional resources;*

- *to the funding bodies that the next Research Assessment Exercise is amended to encourage institutions to make strategic decisions about whether to enter departments for the Exercise or whether to seek a lower level of non-competitive funding to support research and scholarship which underpins teaching;*

- *to the government that an Industrial Partnership Development Fund is established immediately to attract matching funds from industry, and to contribute to regional and economic development;*

- *to the government that it promotes and enables, as soon as possible, the establishment of a revolving loan fund of £400 to £500 million, financed jointly by public and private research sponsors, to support infrastructure in a limited number of top quality research departments which can demonstrate a real need (recommendation 34).*

We recommend that all higher education institutions in the UK should have in place overarching communications and information strategies by 1999/2000 (recommendation 41).

We recommend that all higher education institutions should develop managers who combine a deep understanding of communications and information technology with senior management experience (recommendation 42).

We recommend to the government that it should review existing copyright legislation and consider how it might be amended to facilitate greater ease of use of copyright materials in digital form by teachers and researchers (recommendation 43).

We recommend to the government and the funding bodies that, to harness and maximize the benefits of communications and information technology, they should secure appropriate network connectivity to all sites of higher education delivery and further education colleges by 1999/2000, and to other relevant bodies over the medium term (recommendation 44).

We recommend that institutions of higher education, collectively or individually as appropriate, should negotiate reduced tariffs from telecommunications providers on behalf of students as soon as possible (recommendation 45).

We recommend to institutions that, over the medium term, they develop and implement arrangements which allow staff and external bodies to have access to and understand the true costs of research (recommendation 52).

We recommend that the Committee of Vice-Chancellors and Principals, in collaboration with other institutional representative bodies, reviews the functions of the Universities and Colleges Information Systems Association to ensure that it can promote the implementation of communications and information technology in management information systems (recommendation 53).

We recommend that the government, together with representative bodies, should, within three years, establish whether the identity of the governing body in each institution is clear and undisputed. Where it is not, the government should take action to clarify the position, ensuring that the Council is the ultimate decision-making body, and that the Court has a wider representative role, to inform decision-making but not to take decisions (recommendation 54).

We recommend to the government that it takes action so that:

- *individuals may not serve as members of a governing body for more than two terms, unless they also hold office;*

- *it is a requirement for the governing body at each institution to include student and staff membership and a majority of lay members;*

- *an individual may not chair a governing body for more than two terms of office (recommendation 55).*

We recommend that the government takes the lead, with the Privy Council, in discussions with institutional representatives to introduce, within three years, revised procedures capable of responding more quickly to an institution requesting a change in the size of its governing body. The intention should be to ensure a response within one year (recommendation 56).

We recommend that each governing body should systematically review, at least once every five years, with appropriate external assistance and benchmarks:

- *its own effectiveness and, where there is in excess of 25 members, show good reason why a larger body is needed for its effectiveness;*

- *the arrangements for discharging its obligations to the institution's external constituencies;*

- *all major aspects of the institution's performance, including the participation strategy.*

The outcomes of the review should be published in an institution's annual report. The funding bodies should make such a review a condition of public funding (recommendation 57).

We recommend that, over the medium term, to assist governing bodies in carrying out their systematic reviews funding bodies and representative bodies develop appropriate performance indicators and benchmarks for families of institutions with similar characteristics and aspirations (recommendation 58).

We recommend to the funding bodies that they require institutions, as a condition of public funding, to publish annual reports which describe the outcomes of the governing body's review and report on other aspects of compliance with the code of practice on governance (recommendation 59).

We recommend to institutions that, over the next two years, they review and, if necessary, amend their arrangements for handling complaints from students, to ensure that: they reflect the principles of natural justice; they are transparent and timely; they include procedures for reconciliation and arbitration; they include an independent, external element; and they are managed by a senior member of staff (recommendation 60).

We recommend to the government that, over the long term, public spending on higher education should increase with the growth in Gross Domestic Product (recommendation 71).

We recommend to the government that it shifts the balance of funding, in a planned way, away from block grant towards a system in which funding follows the student, assessing the impact of each successive shift on institutional behaviour and the control of public expenditure, with a target of distributing at least 60 per cent of total public funding to institutions according to student choice by 2003 (recommendation 72).

We recommend to the government that the public funding for higher education institutions should be determined on a rolling three-year basis (recommendation 73).

We recommend to the government that variations in the level of public funding for teaching, outside modest margins, should occur only where:

- *there is an approved difference in the provision;*

- *society, through the Secretary of State or his or her agent, concludes, after examining an exceptionally high level of funding, that in relation to other funding needs in higher education, it represents a good use of resources (recommendation 74).*

We recommend to the funding bodies that they should explore the possibility of setting aside some of their total grant, as soon as possible, to establish revolving loan schemes to fund:

- *projects to refurbish buildings (to improve fitness for purpose) or to undertake large scale long-term maintenance projects;*

- *expensive equipment purchases (for teaching or research);*

- *collaborative projects which will facilitate access for staff and students in a region to teaching or research facilities which could not otherwise be provided on a viable basis (recommendation 75).*

We recommend to the government that the Teacher Training Agency continue its remit in respect of teacher training in England but that the respective responsibilities of the Higher Education Funding Council for England and the Teacher Training Agency are reviewed in drawing up proposals for the role of a General Teaching Council (recommendation 87).

The reaction of the universities to this bundle is again likely to be mixed. A healthy scepticism (born of bitter experience) about the real terms uplift in funding, ought not to disguise welcome for a sensible approach to year-on-year efficiency gains, a longer budgetary planning horizon, and the firm declaration that the new source of income (student fees) should be 'ring-fenced' for the support of institutions. Many in England would have liked to see the Teacher Training Agency swept away (as was indeed the thrust of the specialist report commissioned by Sir Ron from Professor Stewart Sutherland [NCIHE Report 10]); for the Committee, however, this appears to have been a bridge too far.

In other respects the Dearing approach to management, governance and the 'market' in which institutions operate will be seen as carefully balanced. For example, there is a distinctive attempt to restore the role of internal stake-holders in the strategic direction of institutions coupled with a resistance to many of the now external charges against 'new managerialism'. Similarly, a desire to see student 'purchasing power' better reflected in the pattern of provision is matched with devices (like three-year funding) designed to bolster institutional stability.

The details of the package will not be achieved smoothly or easily. Charging for JISC-related services will probably be accepted (given sufficient lead time and appropriate adjustments to grant — in effect the return of at least a part of the top-slice). The research settlement could prove more contentious: general acceptance (and welcome) for the Arts and Humanities Research Council will be coupled with concern about further adjustments to the dual support system (based on a fear that the 'full costs' of Research Council projects will not be met from extra resources but instead from a raid on existing 'R' money). There will also be reluctance by at least some institutions to accept the moral hazard of entering and failing to score in the RAE.

Similarly, we can predict complaints that the recommendations on management and governance are too detailed and intrusive, although many individual vice-chancellors will wish to make immediate use of some of the proposed levers — for example on the size of governing bodies. The CVCP will protest that it is already under way and a post-Nolan exercise on identifying the best processes for handling complaints.

Finally, the progress of Dearing's noted endorsement of the 'market' principle, coupled with the equally circumspect support for level funding for comparable activity, will be watched with care. The former (recommendation 72) perhaps insufficiently recognizes the extent to which funding already follows the market (students recruited bring their local authority fee, and institutions not recruiting to target have their grants 'clawed back'). The latter (recommendation 74) will also be important for what it implies but does not state explicitly: there is no place in the Dearing compact for individually levied 'top-up' fees.

14   Supporting Staff

As the previous two chapters have emphasized, staff of all types within the university have delivered astonishing levels of 'efficiency gains' over the last decade and a half, with apparently little effect on the quality of their product. Quality of life, for all who work in institutions (students as well as staff) is a different issue, and low morale (perhaps as dramatic as misery in some pockets of the system) has been a distinct result. As in schools, a sense is growing that some sort of fresh start is required, and the Dearing Report responds to this in a number of interrelated ways.

Pay and Conditions

There can be quarrels about the specific methodology employed (whether or not it relates to actual earning and incremental effects, for example) but all of the objective evidence points to academic staff within institutions falling dramatically behind their peers and their expectations in terms of personal reward. Figure 14.1 is based upon evidence accumulated by the Association of University Teachers (AUT). Current national agreements on funding pay in both former sectors cannot be said to have served the system well.

In 1997 the unions and the CVCP commissioned an 'Independent Pay Review' headed by Lord Borrie and coordinated by Hay Management Consultants. The purpose was directly to inform the Dearing Committee. Based upon a job-evaluation method, taking posts with similar levels of responsibility, the main conclusions are set out in figure 14.2 below.

The 'post-binary' division indicated here is also reflected in superannuation schemes, where members of the former UFC institutions belong to the fully funded Universities Superannuation Scheme (USS) and members of the former PCFC institutions belong to the national teachers' scheme (TSS), which is based, like national pensions, on receipts meeting current rather than future liabilities. The funding councils adjust their grants to the two types of institutions in order to cover differential employers' contributions to the two schemes.

The differing status of these schemes has led not only to higher rates of benefit for the former, but also to greater flexibility for traditional university management in being able to offer subsidized premature retirement. In the public sector from the end of 1997 almost all such extra costs fall upon the individual institutions rather than the scheme. The huge costs involved in establishing a unified scheme have prevented any real movement on this question, which remains in some ways the most potent legacy of the binary system.

Figure 14.1   Real earnings growth among professional staff, 1981–1992

• Male university teachers	8.6%
• Male FE teachers	9.4%
• Local authority architects etc.	12.9%
• Civil Service tax specialists	13.3%
• Local authority welfare workers	18.8%
• NHS nurses	29.4%
• Male police inspectors	30.1%
• NHS hospital doctors	34.5%
• Male primary and secondary school teachers	35.0%
• Private sector non-manual men	37.1%
• Male fire officers	39.4%

Source: Elliott and Duffus, 1996.

Figure 14.2   Hay review: Selected pay comparisons 1997

Comparator group	University group	'Old' universities % pay related to median	'New' universities % pay related to median
Manual staff	Manual staff	63–103%	67–110%
Public sector	APT & C staff	N/A	74–87%
Private sector	Clerical staff	67%	N/A
Public sector	Clerical staff	79%	N/A
Private sector	Senior admin. (grade 6)	111%	N/A
Public sector	Senior admin. (grade 6)	122%	N/A
Private sector	Academic	70–79%	70–79%
Public sector	Academic	78–81%	78–81%

Source: Hay Management Consultants, 1997.

Consideration of pay cannot, however, be divorced from issues of conditions at national and local level and changing institutional status has complicated and intensified disputes over conditions, most dramatically in the removal of tenure for new appointees to the traditional universities after 1988 (House and

Watson, 1995). There are two special challenges here, picked up by Dearing: the core definition of an academic's role; and the relationship of teaching to other learning support staff. Each should be read as directly relevant to his proposed independent review of pay and conditions.

Staff Development

While it cannot be denied that human resource management in higher education has been significantly enhanced over the past decade, for example with reference to equal opportunities policies, systematic attention to the improvement of the primary teaching function has been patchy. Dearing joins the group that has been lobbying for full-scale professional accreditation of teaching in higher education, and is enthusiastic about both domestic models (as set out by SEDA) and international examples (especially the Netherlands).

The majority of institutions would now claim to have such schemes in place, especially for teachers new to higher education. There are, however, difficulties in assessing the real impact of such commitments. Content naturally varies, as does the approach to quality control and accreditation. The SEDA scheme, which appears to be the market leader, operates by establishing base criteria which each approved provider has to prove it is able to meet, and this seems likely to be the approach favoured by the Institute for Learning and Teaching following Dearing. A CVCP Working Party, informed by a position paper prepared by Jean Bocock, also begins from the premise of a permissive framework (Bocock, 1997).

The Interprofessional Challenge

One effect of increased professionalism in teaching should be the recognition of the range of specialized inputs that go into a successful learning environment: not only teaching and support from librarians and computing personnel, but also good administration and management. For many within the institutions, especially those who wish to emphasize the special status of 'academic' or 'faculty' members, this implies some important cultural changes, to which we return in chapters 19 and 20 below.

The key to the problem, and the solution, lies in interprofessional respect (or the lack of it) and staff development programmes designed to foster such respect. Like most complex organizations, universities and colleges are organized in both formal and informal hierarchies. The modal university hierarchy is set out in figure 14.3. It operates uniformly in descending order of influence, capacity to make noise, and self-esteem.

Precisely how these relationships pan out will depend upon the differing constitutional position of, for example, chartered universities and the higher

Figure 14.3   The university hierarchy

- Principal or Vice-Chancellor

- Other 'management'

- 'Academic' teaching staff (or 'faculty')

- Professional support staff

- Technical staff

- Clerical staff

- Manual staff

education corporations (HECs). In the former there is often a strict demarcation (almost reminiscent of *apartheid*) between 'faculty' and 'administration'. In the latter there is the unexpected historical democratization of all having at one stage been employees of the local authority.

The critical issue in establishing appropriate teamwork is the danger of privileging one viewpoint. It is ironic, for example, in discussions of professionalism that many of the apparently subordinate layers (like librarians and finance staff) have 'imported' professional models and status to rely upon, while in contrast 'the academic profession is probably *unprofessional*, especially in its orientation to teaching' (Fulton, 1993). Efforts to merge pay-scales across the different professional areas, to move to a single spine of pay points, and to establish a uniform job-evaluation system have so far all proved contentious and unproductive (see for example the fate of the Fender Report, *Promoting People*, of 1993 — after an initial flurry of enthusiasm it has sunk without trace) (CVCP, 1993).

Responding to Dearing

The key relevant recommendations are as follows:

We recommend that all institutions should, over the medium term, review the changing role of staff as a result of communications and information technology, and ensure that staff and students receive appropriate training and support to enable them to realize its full potential (recommendation 9).

We recommend that institutions of higher education begin immediately to develop or seek access to programmes for teacher training of their staff, if they do not have them, and that all institutions seek national accreditation of such programmes from the Institute for Learning and Teaching in Higher Education (recommendation 13).

We recommend that, over the next year, all institutions should:

- *review and update their staff development policies to ensure they address the changing roles of staff;*

- *publish their policies and make them readily available for all staff;*

- *consider whether to seek the Investors in People award (recommendation 47).*

We recommend to institutions that, over the medium term, it should become the normal requirement that all new full-time academic staff with teaching responsibilities are required to achieve at least associate membership of the Institute for Learning and Teaching in Higher Education, for the successful completion of probation (recommendation 48).

We recommend that all institutions should, as part of their human resources policy, maintain equal opportunities policies, and, over the medium term, should identify and remove barriers which inhibit recruitment and progression for particular groups and monitor and publish their progress towards greater equality of opportunity for all groups (recommendation 49).

We recommend to the higher education employers that they appoint, after consultation with staff representatives, an independent review committee to report by April 1998 on the framework for determining pay and conditions of service. The Chairman should be appointed on the nomination of the government (recommendation 50).

We recommend to the government, institutions, and the representative bodies of higher education, that, over the long term, the superannuation arrangements for academic staff should be harmonized by directing all new entrants to the Universities Superannuation Scheme (recommendation 51).

At one level institutions, and staff, should have little difficulty in signing up to this essentially exhortatory set of recommendations. Beneath the surface, however, some real difficulties emerge. For example, the staff profile has not developed to match the increasing diversity of the student body. The latest statistics from the CVCP indicate that only 29 per cent of university staff are female, and only 9 per cent of the professorial grade and above (CVCP, 1997a). Dearing also discovered that only one-third of the majority of institutions with equal opportunities policies had plans directed towards their achievement.

Similarly, teacher professionalism — if it is to be embedded within a professional institute (along the lines of the General Medical Council or a General Teaching Council) — will raise difficult questions for a traditionally unionized sector about professional standards and discipline.

The other injunctions about the context of staff development (especially in support of C and IT) should prove less contentious, while review of pay and conditions and harmonization of superannuation (provided the government is able to agree to the knock-on costs of the latter) will be generally welcomed. Staff should, however, beware of premature celebration. The review body will be presented not only with evidence of university staff falling behind but also with the fact that the sector has experienced no major problems of recruitment or retention.

From the perspective of lifelong learning, the key is likely to be the extent to which the programmes and policies set out for staff development and teacher accreditation will take account of the special needs of adult and 'returning' students.

15　Supporting Communities

In 1994 the Committee of Vice-Chancellors and Principals published a report on *Universities and Communities* (CVCP, 1994). This was a significant document in several respects. Traditionally, universities have regarded themselves as having a national and international focus and have paid scant attention to their localities and regions. Student recruitment, at least in the traditional universities of England and Wales, has been very largely national (and full-time); postgraduate students have been recruited increasingly internationally as well as nationally; and research has been conducted within an international context. All these trends have been increasingly dominant in the post-war period although the historical roots of many of these universities were, paradoxically, precisely in their localities. (The prime examples here are, of course, the large civic universities, such as Leeds, Manchester, Birmingham and Sheffield.)

Local Links

In recent years, however, these trends have altered significantly. All universities now acknowledge the importance of their local and regional communities. This applies in particular to the new universities whose origins, missions, student bodies and overall culture remain in most cases very strongly local. But it also applies to many traditional universities. As the CVCP document makes clear, 'universities are an important growth element in regional economies'. The new universities are far more locally oriented in terms of student recruitment; about half of the old universities estimate that they recruit less than 20 per cent of their students from the local area, while half of the new universities recruit over 40 per cent locally. Virtually all universities refer in their institutional plans to the need for good relations and partnerships with their local communities, although only 47 per cent of traditional universities regard this as a high priority, compared with 74 per cent of new universities (ibid., pp. 1–4).

Activities highlighted in the CVCP report include technology transfer, the built environment, local economic development, social and community links, tourism and conferencing, and cultural developments (university involvement in arts centres and the like). There is also recognition of the university role as both an investor, and a facilitator of others' investment as in science parks and (more recently) small-scale incubator units for 'spin-out' and 'new start' high technology firms.

The report advocates active, strategic development of university/community links, with each area of activity having 'a clearly identified "socket" within the university into which individuals and organizations in the local community can plug'. Local authorities are seen as the most appropriate agencies to bring together the various private, public and voluntary sector organizations in the community, in partnership with the university (ibid.).

There is thus a new priority for universities, as evidenced in the CVCP document, for local and regional activities and partnerships. Similar themes have emerged from a follow-up study conducted by McNicoll (McNicoll, 1995). However, important though these developments are, the conception of 'community' assumed in the CVCP document concentrates largely upon employers, industry, local government agencies and so on albeit with brief reference to adult education, access, and cultural activities. This emphasis is also echoed in key sections of the Dearing Report, especially in the context of matching funding for locally-based research and development (as in the proposed Industrial Partnership Development Fund) (NCIHE, 1997, Main Report, Chapter 12). There is little if any evidence of concern with local communities *per se* — in terms of the local workforce and its representative organizations, and the large proportion of the population who have not been involved with any education since leaving school. (After all, even the envisaged mass higher education system is planned to involve a participation rate of 40–45 per cent.)

Continuing Education and the Community

In some ways, therefore, concern with the local and regional community has been integrated within the traditional, elitist culture of the university system. But this has not been a total, monolithic culture — and it is becoming rapidly less so as the transition to a mass higher education system proceeds apace. Historically, continuing education provision has had a central concern with local communities; and, in the evolving, contemporary HE system the move to a lifelong learning system is essentially and systemically based in the community concept.

CE, in the traditional university system, operated both as an external agency and as a deviant sub-culture whereby the universities were able, at little cost and without interference with their mainstream activities, to maintain educational contact with their local population and with local organizations. The philosophy underpinning such provision was, and has been well-documented and discussed (see Taylor, et al., 1985; Wallis, 1995), the 'liberal tradition'. Although much of the emphasis within this context was upon personal development, within an individualistic ideology stemming from liberalism, there has also been a strong and persistent 'social purpose' strand to CE (Fieldhouse, 1996; Ward and Taylor, 1986; Thompson and Mayo, 1996). It is this dimension which is especially relevant to the analysis of the present and future roles of universities in relation to their communities. If lifelong learning, in the emerging context of the mass HE system, is to have real purchase upon the whole of society rather than only its elite, then the experience and culture of social purpose CE must be integrated within it.

Social purpose CE has had two primary focuses of interest and provision: industrial studies for working-class, trade union students; and community education for disadvantaged groups such as unemployed people, working-class women and retired people, and ethnic minorities. Trade unions and the Labour Movement are deeply unfashionable in these New Labour, post-modernist times. It is thus doubly necessary for their importance and educational relevance to be stressed; not only do approximately eight million employees belong to trade unions, there is a long experience of educational partnership between universities and individual unions, and the TUC. This has been a long and often contentious relationship (McIlroy, 1985, 1988; Holford, 1994) for reasons of both pedagogy and politics. The work has been characterized, however, by universities' sensitivity to the competing demands for vocationalism and liberal education. To balance these requirements has been difficult in a context where study time is both short and competing with other demands on students. There is also the added pedagogical problem that the large majority of trade union students have left school at the minimum age with few or no qualifications, little experience of study skills, and often with a negative experience of school education.

The continuous, large scale success of such provision through the decades from the end of the war until the 1980s was remarkable, and more importantly could act as a basis for lifelong learning development between universities and trade unions in the new environment. The network of contacts, the pedagogical structures, the mutual understanding and trust, are all important elements in the existing and historical relationship. Even more important are the curriculum approaches embodied in such trade union work. Some schemes, such as the large scale 'Health and Safety' provision through the TUC, have been relatively low-level and specific in their approach and purpose (and were delivered largely through the WEA and FE system). However, even here there was opportunity for 'liberal' approaches to be included in the actual delivery. Others, such as the long — usually three year — day release courses for specific unions such as the miners, engineers, steel workers or, more recently, white-collar workers, were wide-ranging in their coverage. A typical syllabus for the latter type of course would include generic support elements — study skills, communication, and so on — as well as relevant disciplinary programmes. The focus for such programmes was the study and analysis of the worker, the union, and the labour movement in the context of the wider society and its structure and processes. There would thus be sections on labour history and politics, industrial sociology, micro and macro economics, and the opportunity to study in more depth industrial relations, particularly in the specific industry concerned.

The progress of some of the more able students on courses such as these was outstanding in terms of what would now be termed 'added value'. Many went on successfully to university, or to one of the adult residential colleges, and many more returned to pursue useful and politically radical careers in the industrial and political labour movement.

The environment has of course changed radically and there are few if any of these types of courses now provided. But there are several examples of adapting the structure, while preserving the curriculum approaches, for trade union students which could be used as the basis for large scale expansion as part of a lifelong learning system. Distance Learning (DL) schemes, based on paper package systems or on IT methods or a mix of the two, have been launched very successfully over the last few years. (The Leeds programmes with the TGWU and UNISON are two which have attracted national attention.) It is important, given the study skills needs and lack of educational experience of the students concerned, for there to be substantial elements of face-to-face seminar work to complement the DL provision.

Closely related to these developments is the growing field of work-based learning. Although currently small-scale WBL has huge potential. Most work at present is concentrated upon NVQ Levels 3, 4 and 5 or their equivalents and upon large companies where IT infrastructures and staff training and development systems are all in place. WBL for trade unionists and other working class employees is under-developed and offers a challenging opportunity for universities. The curriculum and pedagogy used now on a small scale with the programmes for trade unionists in DL settings could be adopted for WBL purposes and could involve very large numbers of students, studying mostly in the workplace and at home rather than on campus. The mix of the vocational and liberal which characterized the old TU day release programmes could be used, with content and approach revised as necessary, to form the basis of such provision. The specialist pedagogical expertise exists in the full-time and part-time staff of the CE system to ensure quality and effectiveness and equally importantly to guarantee trust and understanding between the very different worlds of HE and the workplace.

The most difficult problems with such proposed development may well be financial and administrative. One of the attractions of postgraduate level WBL provision is its relative cheapness because so much of the work can be legitimately project-based and company-related. Trade union-related WBL is inescapably more expensive and there are also administrative problems — over IT access, over face-to-face seminar arrangements, and over curriculum 'realignment' by HEIs. None of these is insuperable, however, if there is commitment from HE, trade unions and the TUC, and not least the government.

The other main plank of social purpose CE has been community education. Its roots lie in the 1960s and 1970s, partly in community work and more generally radical social work, and partly in the movement for radical, libertarian local activism designed to empower 'ordinary people' to take control over their lives and their communities (Ward and Taylor, 1986; Lovett, 1975, 1988). The development of CE initiatives in this area were supported by the RB grant system for adult education departments which, backed often by HMI, permitted such provision. Much depended on local circumstances but, in many of the big urban conurbations — Birmingham, Leeds and Sheffield for example — universities were encouraged by HMI to develop innovative community provision. Organizationally, this was facilitated by a plethora of usually small-scale developmental grant schemes, REPLAN being perhaps the most notable.

There were a number of key characteristics of such provision, many of which are relevant to the development of the lifelong learning system. Provision is almost always based in the community not the institution. This has been a key factor in involving groups and individuals for whom the world of universities — and even FE — is seen as irrelevant if not alien. The persistent image of the university amongst the bulk of the population remains, with some justification, middle-class and unconnected with everyday realities. Provision is best located in familiar local surroundings — community centres and the like — and organized and recruited for on an informal basis. Secondly, curriculum design and delivery needs sophisticated team planning. Approaches have varied. In Liverpool in the 1970s, for example, successful provision was organized around traditional disciplinary areas — social studies, literature — mainly for committed community activists. In the rather special circumstances of Northern Ireland, Tom Lovett and others have developed a series of community action, community issue programmes (Lovett, 1975, 1988). In Birmingham, a large programme oriented to the ethnic minority communities was provided in the 1970s and 1980s, primarily in the cultural and social studies areas. In Leeds, the University organized a large programme of issue-based provision oriented to unemployed people, women's groups, ethnic minorities, and the working-class retired communities (Ward and Taylor, 1986).

The success of the programmes depended in part upon recasting the curriculum to make academic disciplines of relevance to the targeted disadvantaged communities. In the Leeds programme, for example, all curriculum was 'deconstructed' and reassembled to address real issues of perceived relevance: rather than 'social policy', for example, short courses on 'welfare rights' or 'housing' were provided. The aim — not always achieved — was to link these applied courses to the wider sociological and political context and thus introduce students to at least some of the relevant disciplinary frameworks.

A third characteristic of such provision has been its partnership basis. Almost all successful provision of community education has been organized as a partnership between the university and the LEA, FE college, voluntary body (tenants' association, unemployed centre, ethnic minority group etc.), trade union or some other similar body. This is partly for practical reasons — appropriate accommodation, local knowledge and so on — but also for 'philosophical' reasons. For community education to be successful it must arise from a genuine dialogue between the community and the university, and not be imposed by the university. It is not a question of the university offering its provision on a 'take-it-or-leave-it' basis, rather, the university must adapt and develop its provision to meet the needs of the community. There are of course important quality assurance issues to be addressed, as discussed in chapter 11. But the essential point is that only on a partnership basis can a genuinely community education provision be made.

Again, these experiences are germane to the development of a full lifelong learning system: they are also of course related closely to the need for developing full cooperation with FE (as discussed in a more general context in chapter 16).

The modular, credited rated structure of a potential mass HE system is the ideal context for implementing these CE modes of learning. With appropriate FE/HE/voluntary sector partnerships, community education defined broadly could be an integral part of the new system of lifelong learning. Such development will be made increasingly easy by two additional factors: the practice and experience of the new universities and some of the former CAT institutions in the provision of vocational courses, and part-time degree and pre-degree level programmes for adults from their localities; and the new Labour government's emphasis upon the development of coordinated regional educational provision in the post-compulsory sector (and, even more, of formal devolution in Scotland and Wales). Finally, it is important that employers should be encouraged to work closely with these structures to ensure that all employees have access to recognized education and training opportunities.

Responding to Dearing

Dearing unambiguously buys the argument for a regional dimension in the development of HE, expressed in terms of research and consultancy, training needs, and , in a lower key, general cultural contribution. However, it could be argued that the Report fails to address both the detail of a workable regional system and some of the difficult political issues, including institutional autonomy and of how best to reconcile national funding and policy regimes with regional power.

The key relevant recommendations are as follows:

We recommend to the government that institutions of higher education should be represented on the regional bodies which it establishes, and that the Further Education Funding Council regional committees should include a member from higher education (recommendation 36).

We recommend to the government that funding should continue to be available after April 1998, when the present provision from the Higher Education Regional Development Fund is due to cease, to support human capital projects which enable higher education to be responsive to the needs of local industry and commerce (recommendation 37).

We recommend to higher education institutions and their representative bodies that they examine, with representatives of industry, ways of giving firms, especially small and medium sized enterprises, easy and coordinated access to information about higher education services in their area (recommendation 38).

We recommend:

- *to the government that it considers establishing a modest fund to provide equity funding to institutions to support members of staff or students in taking forward business ideas developed in the institution, and to support the creation of incubator units;*

- *to higher education institutions that they establish more technology incubator units within or close to the institution, within which start-up companies can be fostered for a limited period until they are able to stand alone (recommendation 39).*

This set of ideas from the Dearing Committee stresses the economic role of higher education rather than any wider social or cultural concerns. It is, however, likely to be in tune with key aspects of the Labour government programme, particularly on regional development. Specific ideas about links with SMEs and 'incubator' units will be welcomed by those universities already involved in such initiatives (for example through Teaching Company Schemes and Business Links).

The major uncertainty, however, is how further and higher education will be represented on or by Regional Development Agencies, and especially how regional training strategies (including the government's 'welfare-to-work' programme funded by a windfall tax on the privatized utilities) will work out through the current Parliament.

16 Supporting the State

The Dearing Report, like Robbins, is unequivocal about the role of higher education as a national asset. What is more, it attempts to justify rather than merely assert this claim. While recommending continuation of the historical pattern of independence from supervision and direction of the state (and hence also of 'academic freedom' in the best sense of that term), the Report also recognizes the essential 'fit' between higher and further education and the compulsory phase, and tries to be sensitive to the particular requirements of the 'territories' (Scotland, Wales and Northern Ireland). Finally, there is a strong suggestion that the nation should not be made to wait another 30 years before it receives expert advice on the legitimate expectations from a relevant system of higher education.

Historically, universities have remained somewhat aloof from discussions couched in these terms, except at the highest level of generality. Defensive assertion of their importance to the state, civil society and the economy has outweighed analysis and reasoned argument, while the struggle over 'accountability' (see chapter 11 above) has added to the tension.

Post-compulsory Frameworks and Policies

As indicated in our elaboration of the administrative context in which the UK higher education context is managed, the Conservative government of 1979–97 was ruthless in terms of the speed and comprehensiveness with which they were prepared to bring about change. At no stage, however, did they fundamentally question the principle of intermediary or 'buffer' bodies having responsibility for direct funding allocations to institutions. Despite the strength of whatever 'steer' the Secretary of State of the day was pre-disposed to give to the funding councils (and from time to time such 'instruction' was very direct — for example on expansion or 'consolidation', or the protection or otherwise of research funding), the principle of institutional autonomy was formally maintained.

Dearing notes this, as well as its contrast with the more direct state control and intervention in many other countries of the European Union, and endorses its continuation (NCIHE, 1997, Main Report, Chapter 22). He does, however, also underline how much this privileged position depends on public trust, and a number of ways in which collective self-discipline (that is, the autonomous institutions deciding to act together and taking mutual responsibility for the outcomes) is vital. These include not only standards and quality assurance, but also public information and promotion (including institutional titles) (NCIHE, 1997, Main Report 16.15–31).

One particularly sensitive point in the national framework is the boundary between further and higher education, on which currently slightly different administrative and funding arrangements occur in each of the territories of the UK. Dearing again goes with the grain of the current arrangements, modified only (as in Northern Ireland and Scotland) where there is clear local preference for a modified development. However, this should not disguise the strength, and potentially radical nature of his overall recommendations on higher education in further education colleges (HE in FE).

In practice the boundary between the two sectors has become blurred as a result of several developments: public funding for access or 'foundation year' courses in both HEIs and FEIs (and funded by both Further and Higher Education Funding Councils); FEIs achieving licences from BTEC (now Edexcel) to award both HNCs and HNDs; and agreements ('validation' and 'franchising') to offer the early part of degree courses into FE colleges. A study by Jean Bocock and Peter Scott elaborates the effects of this blurred boundary on provision in the FE sector, including the potentially isolated nature of the experience of 'degree' students in FE (Bocock and Scott, 1994). While this pattern may serve the cause of lifelong learning in some respects, it also causes difficulties of quality assurance, of mission drift within FE (Dearing is especially worried about entrepreneurial 'multiple' franchising relationships between a single FEI and a range of HEIs), and of information to students.

The Dearing Report attempts to tackle these by offering a clear and important mission for FE in HE, structured around the expansion the Committee would like to see in sub-degree work (especially HNDs). The example of Scotland, where the advance of the APR to approximately 45 per cent is significantly a product of (directly funded) HNCs and HNDs in further education colleges, was influential on this decision (NCIHE, 1997, Main Report 7.30). The corollary, of a progressive disengagement from degree work in FE, except under circumstances in which the awarding HEI takes direct responsibility for delivery, standards and quality, is likely to lead to much heart-searching (ibid., Main Report 16.39–41). It is, however, consistent with the Committee's other views on the distinctiveness of higher education alluded to in chapter 8 above.

Higher Education as an International Business

The commissioners of the Dearing Report were as conscious of the reputation and role of UK higher education internationally as they were of the sensitivities surrounding its national status. The terms of reference for the Committee pointed to the standing of UK qualifications 'throughout the world', 'competitive international markets' and the pace of change elsewhere. They thus caught a mood of uneasy pride in this aspect of the UK's global performance, and concern that international leadership might be under threat.

Strong perceived advantages of the UK system in the global context, all acknowledged in the Main Report including its historical legacy and reputation, making Britain an important *entrepôt* for cultural exchange, the primacy of the English language, an extraordinary rate of research production and effect, and special features like the communications network (JANET and SuperJANET) which links all domestic HEIs and thus opens up the rest of the world to the system collectively. Simultaneously there is a fear of falling behind, as other countries (the 'Asian tigers' as well as the rest of Europe) set and achieve higher targets for participation (the former particularly), or seem poised (especially North America) to tackle global markets for advanced distance learning. There is also suspicion that research leadership is fragile, and that the current favourable indicators (of citation and impact) are the products of a 'lag' from an earlier, more generously funded regime.

More specific problems include concerns over quality control of international franchising (especially the market impact of negative reports from British agencies, which can turn the asset of strict quality control into a short-term dilution of reputation), uncertainties over the comparative standards of awards (with consequent difficulties for professional recognition in an international context), the long lamented weakness of the UK science base in technology transfer and exchange, and the competitiveness in an international market of UK academic salaries. All of these are matters potentially addressed and ameliorated by specific domestic recommendations and reforms, but the new global market of increased trade activity across traditional boundaries and especially the late twentieth century phenomenon of the global company (the 'footloose corporation') give them added urgency.

It is, of course, not only reputation at stake. Higher education is now a tradeable commodity and a UK market lead (the CVCP estimates that approximately £1 billion of additional spending is generated by international students and overseas contracts held by universities and colleges) can no longer be assumed. In response, and in addition to simply trying harder on the initiatives set out above, Dearing also makes positive recommendations on benchmarking (the international membership of both QAA and RAE processes discussed in chapter 11) and on adding to our national research ambitions the goal of becoming 'the world leader in the practice of teaching at higher levels' (ibid., Main Report 8.76).

The Next Dearing?

The Dearing Committee was established in an atmosphere of crisis, and the political discussion of its recommendations at the time of writing has done little to dispel the tension or the uncertainty. This raises some interesting questions about the national stewardship of higher education: who is responsible for the ongoing health of the system as a whole (as opposed to the individual institutions which make it up)? Like the Paul Hamlyn National Commission on Education before it (which had a wider remit), the Dearing Committee is concerned about the quality and quantity of relevant research being conducted by the Department for Education and Employment, and its capacity for posing policy options in a measured and informed way (National Commission on Education, 1993). The outcome is a suggestion that we should not have to wait another third of a century for another Dearing, especially in the context of the rapid social, economic and educational changes anticipated.

Responding to Dearing

The key relevant recommendations are as follows:

We recommend to the government that it should establish, as soon as possible, a high level independent body to advise the government on the direction of national policies for the public funding of research in higher education, on the distribution and level of such funding, and on the performance of the public bodies responsible for distributing it (recommendation 35).

We recommend to the government that it takes action as soon as possible to end the scope for a confusion between the title and the name used by institutions, either through clarifying the legal position or by ensuring that conditions can be placed on the flow of public funds so that these go only to those institutions which agree to restrict their use of a name and title to that to which they are legally entitled (recommendation 62).

We recommend to the government that, in the medium term, there is no change to the current criteria for university status; but that, for the future, there should be a period of relative stability in the number of universities with the weight accorded to the numerical criteria reduced and greater emphasis placed on a distinctive role and characteristics in awarding this status; and that the government should give notice of this (recommendation 63).

We recommend to the government that it takes action, either by clarifying the legal position or by ensuring that conditions can be placed on the flow of public funds, to restrict the use of the title 'University College' to those institutions which are in every sense a college which is part of a university under the control of the university's governing body; and to those higher education institutions which have been granted taught degree awarding powers (recommendation 65).

We recommend to the government and the funding bodies that there is greater clarity about where responsibility lies for decisions about the establishment of new universities; and that criteria are developed for deciding such cases and allocating public funding (recommendation 66).

We recommend to the government and the funding bodies that, in the medium term, priority in growth in sub-degree provision should be accorded to further education colleges; and that, wherever possible:

- *more sub-degree provision should take place in further education colleges;*

- *higher education provision in further education colleges should be funded directly;*

- *there should be no growth in degree level qualifications offered by further education colleges (recommendation 67).*

We recommend to the government that Scottish students who have had only one year's education after statutory schooling, many of whom under current arrangements would choose to take a four-year honours degree, should not make a tuition contribution for one of their years in higher education. Beyond that, this would be a matter for consideration by the Secretary of State for Scotland (recommendation 81).

We recommend to the government that the tradition of institutional separation from national and sub-national levels of government is firmly maintained; and that this principle is extended to Northern Ireland (recommendation 84).

We recommend to the government that the division of responsibility between the further and higher education funding bodies in England and Wales should be such that the higher education funding bodies are responsible for funding all provision defined as higher education (recommendation 86).

We recommend to the government that, in five years' time and subsequently every 10 years, it constitutes a UK-wide independent advisory committee with the task of assessing the state of higher education; advising the government on its financing and on ways in which, in future years, it can best respond to national needs; on any action that may be needed to safeguard the character and autonomy of institutions; and, in particular, on any changes required in the level of student support and contributions from graduates in employment (recommendation 88).

We recommend that higher education institutions in Northern Ireland, in close collaboration with all the relevant external players, steadily enhance their regional role, taking full advantage of the special potential for the development of strong regional networks (recommendation 89).

We recommend to the government that options be examined for substantially increasing the number of higher education places in Northern Ireland in a cost-effective way which involves no compromise in quality and standards (recommendation 90).

We recommend to the government and institutions that consideration be given to adopting the Dearing 16–19-year-olds option as one of the bases for entrance to universities in Northern Ireland (recommendation 91).

We recommend to the government that the scale and nature of funding for research in Northern Ireland universities should be assessed afresh in the context of the Province's strategy for economic development and of the recommendations in chapter 11 (of the Dearing Report) (recommendation 92).

We recommend to the government that there be constituted in Northern Ireland a Tertiary Education Forum, a Higher Education Funding Council and a Further Education Funding Council (recommendation 93).

Making sense of the 'territorial' question in the UK is possibly one of the most serious short-term political questions faced by the Dearing Committee, not least in the context of the September 1997 decisions on devolution. The Committee's Report shows both sympathy and (perhaps too much) deference to the local traditions and preferences of the regions outside of England. Certainly it never tackled frontally the question of differential public funding for major public services (pre-eminently education) that has come to be reflected in the patterns of provision (especially in Scotland) and vigorously defended in a chapter of the Main Report as well as the separate report of the Scottish Committee (NCIHE, 1997, Main Report, Chapter 23; Report of the Scottish Committee).

The Scottish Committee's 29 independent recommendations reflect a mixture of separate, almost competing elements: defensive positioning (especially on the funding of four-year degree programmes, and the need to sort out articulation with parallel but incomplete reforms in secondary education including 'Advanced Higher' proposals); local reform (as in a recommendation that the ancient office of Rector be no longer linked to the Chairmanship of the University Court); and concerns to participate in national initiatives (such as quality and the Institute of Learning and Teaching). (NCIHE, 1997, Report of the Scottish Committee, recommendations 5, 8, 20 and 29.) Their solution to the funding council dilemma is to have two separate agencies (for HE and FE) 'but under a single organization and with a single chief executive' (recommendation 23).

The Report's approach to the Whitehall jungle is equally circumspect. Government departments (including the DfEE) have never been afraid or embarrassed about criticizing higher education (or indeed any other sector of the education service). They have been notoriously reluctant to criticize themselves, or indeed to commission or participate in the kind of research or review that would assist healthy self-criticism. If acted upon, the Dearing proposal of an advisory committee could be of significant service.

Part 5

Impact

17 Lifelong Learning and the World of Work

Lifelong learning and higher education are regarded by the Dearing authors, as they are by the political parties commissioning the Report, as indispensable to economic progress. This proposition has always proved a divisive one for the university culture, but it is hard to suggest that the key arguments have not been won.

Higher Education, 'Enterprise' and 'Competitiveness'

As noted above (chapter 2), the 1980s and 1990s saw several initiatives directed towards increased awareness by staff and students of the needs of the economy, and increased 'work-readiness' by graduates and others leaving higher education. At least some of these programmes (chiefly bank-rolled by the Departments for Employment, before its merger with Education, and the Department of Trade and Industry) went native, but the overall evaluation of their success in terms of increasing economic sensitivity is convincing (Biggs et al., 1994). Perhaps most important in achieving such goals was the effect simply of some extra resources, available to academic managers and staff for initiatives which were manifestly 'extras', and not lost in the relentless fight against the degradation of the unit of resource.

Work Experience

Links with business and industry are, of course, already a mainstream activity for much of higher education, achieved through short and long-term student placements, the 'sandwich' mode of study, use of commerce and industry to provide 'live' case-study and project material, and at the research level the various linked awards and schemes (such as LINK and CASE studentships and, pre-eminently the Teaching Company Scheme). At the level of principle these are widely endorsed by both sides. Dearing records that '[t]he strongest message conveyed to us by employers in the course of all of our work is that they would like more students to have work experience' (NCIHE, 1997, Main Report 3.54).

There are, however, no formal incentives for employers to play, especially at the undergraduate level, as there are in other countries (the Netherlands for example has a scheme of ministry subsidy for SMEs hosting final year under-graduates for their compulsory projects) (ibid., Appendix 5). As a result good-will can come to be defeated, for example in periods of recession when jobs are under threat (sandwich courses linked with the construction industry suffered acutely during the early 1990s). Equally, institutions have sometimes been slow to exercise proper quality control over the experience of students on placement.

The large numbers of mature students in undergraduate programmes, as well as full and part-time students in postgraduate and post-experience courses, of course, already have concurrent and prior work experience.

Graduate Prospects

Prophets of educational and economic doom, like the former Minister of State with responsibility for higher education, Eric Forth, have worried intensely about the effects of expansion in at least two directions: the maintenance of quality and standards (see chapter 11 above), and the potential swamping of the employment market by ill-prepared and consequently disaffected gradu-ates (Forth, 1997). Dearing takes a bolder approach to both questions. On graduate opportunities there is explicit recognition of widespread up-skilling as a social investment, by the nation in its future. Even if graduates do go into jobs that have previously been undertaken by non-graduates, they are there to grow those jobs, to realize the educational dividend of having a more sophis-ticated, adaptable and aware work-force.

Such hopes may appear naively optimistic to graduates stuck in unreward-ing apparently dead-end jobs but they represent an important act of faith on the part of advocates of mass higher education (for a contrary view see Brown and Scase, 1997). Objectively they receive some support from the evidence of high, and only marginally reducing, private rates of return for former students on their investment in higher education. It is also part of Dearing's case for continuing demand for higher education:

> [h]igher education has proved to be an excellent personal investment with a return averaging between 11 and 14 per cent and we expect it to continue to be a good investment, even after further expansion. (NCIHE, 1997, Summary Report, 25)

National Investment

Allied to this discussion is the concept of a 'social' or collective rate of return to the investment made in higher education. Dearing agonized over this ques-tion, and in the process revealed profound disagreement among the ranks of the professional economists. In the end it emerged almost as an article of faith that higher participation, and an approach to lifelong learning encompassing the higher education phase was a sensible national response to economic imperatives. The supporting arguments are almost all contextual: the increasing global interdependence of business activity, the ambitious educational plans of competitor nations and regions, and the diversification of options for those making location decisions about research and development.

Partnerships

Making graduates and the other products of higher education fit for work is, however, a two-way street. The various lists of graduate requirements, linked with the development of 'skills' within the curriculum (discussed in chapter 8) have arguably been absorbed (at least in principle) within the academy. Partly this has been a defensive response to a perennial charge (it waxes and wanes in intensity, but has always been there from the Royal Commissions of Education of the nineteenth century onwards) that education is not delivering 'what employers want'. Partly it is a more positive and active manifestation of the tradition of professional higher education discussed in chapter 10.

Objectively, each side can be accused of at least an element of bad faith. There has been a sense of reluctance by teachers and course designers to be specific about 'embedded' skills in particular in a way that employers (and students) can recognize. Equally, there is certainly a gap between how employers say they will respond to curriculum innovation and what they do; much more recruitment is conducted on a basis of where the candidate studies, rather than what or how they studied, than groups like the Association of Graduate Recruiters (AGR) would like to admit.

Various groups have sprung up in an attempt to deepen and facilitate this debate. One of the most interesting and effective has been the Council for Industry and Higher Education (CIHE). In early 1996 the CIHE convened a meeting of all of the main 'provider' and 'consumer' groups to produce a 'process for moving ahead towards an agreed goal' of 'most (if not all) students to acquire generic employment skills in the course of their first degrees or diplomas'. The signatories to this compact include representatives of CVCP, SCOP, the three funding councils, the DfEE, the TEC National Council, the AGR and Association of Graduate Careers Advisory Service (AGCAS). Their statement includes the following, admirably balanced aim:

> the prior need is for employers to try to describe the future working world as clearly as they can and the demands it seems likely to make on those who are to thrive in it, create opportunities and adapt to change. Correspondingly it will be for academics, from professional knowledge, experience and experiment to describe what may be teachable and learnable within higher education. (CIHE, 1996a)

Responding to Dearing

The key relevant recommendations from the Dearing Inquiry are in the same mould:

We recommend that all institutions should, over the medium term, identify opportunities to increase the extent to which programmes help students to become familiar with work, and help them to reflect on such experience (recommendation 18).

We recommend that companies should take a strategic view of their relationship with higher education and apply the same level of planning to it that they give to other aspects of their operations (recommendation 30).

For many commentators, including probably influential institutional representatives, these recommendations will appear as no more than a feeble stimulus to employers to get involved in higher education. Other recommendations covered in chapters 9 and 15 are also relevant, but it remains true that Dearing (like the National Commission on Education before him) has proved reluctant to establish structural incentives and sanctions on employers to contribute financially to higher education or training. It will be interesting to see whether such critics are right to identify this as potentially the weakest component of the new compact.

18 Lifelong Learning and the Common Culture

The case for the development of a lifelong learning system in higher education is as strong socially as it is economically. Frank Coffield and Bill Williamson put succinctly one important aspect of this argument: '. . . the modern *economic imperative* — that dominant discourse of gaining a competitive edge over "rivals" who used to be called "trading partners" — tells only half the story. It needs to be matched by a *democratic imperative*, which argues that a learning society worthy of the name ought to deliver social cohesion and social justice as well as economic prosperity to *all* its citizens' (Coffield and Williamson, 1997, pp. 2–3). Much of this section pursues this theme.

Higher Education and Social Change

However, there are also broader social factors which have created an environment where the expansion of higher education has become essential. It would be mistaken to view higher education as discrete in this context. As the Kennedy Report on further education has made clear, there is perhaps even greater urgency over FE expansion (Kennedy, 1997). This confirms the analysis of the 1993 Report of the National Commission on Education: '[t]he most serious shortcoming of education . . . is its failure to enable not just a minority but a large majority of young people to obtain as much from their education as they are capable of achieving' (NCE, 1993, p. 2).

It is thus appropriate to begin with the 'social case' for the expansion of post-compulsory education and training (PCET) overall, albeit with a concentration upon higher education. The fundamental drive for the increasing provision of PCET has been economic, as argued in the previous chapter, but this has been strongly buttressed by a range of social factors. The growth of the information and knowledge-based society is a key factor in employment patterns, but it is also important in determining social aspirations. In particular, the pervasive influence of television and increasingly of computer-based information systems — the Internet et al. — have given the generations that have grown up since the 1960s broader horizons and greater expectations. More importantly, the links between job security and income, and educational qualifications have become very clear. During the 1980s and 1990s the real income of the bottom one-fifth of households changed hardly at all whereas it increased by over 20 per cent for the middle fifth and 40 per cent for the top fifth (ibid., p. 20). As indicated in chapter 4, despite the expansion of HE the percentage of entrants from broadly working-class backgrounds has hardly changed since before the war, and the recent rapid expansion has exacerbated rather than resolved the educational inequalities between social classes.

Both geographical mobility and the pace of change in employment have increased markedly: relatively few people can now expect to remain in the same job for life and on average four or five significant job changes can be expected in a normal career. Most employees will come to regard as the norm continuous post-experience education and training. As Chris Duke (1997) has pointed out:

> The idea of graduating to an inalienable status (a 'first class Oxford man') is out of sorts with the idea of lifelong learning: with the fact that adults must and do continue to learn and change as their world changes, through most of their life; and with the facts of technological change and the obsolescence of knowledge, skills and cultural attitudes and values. (p. 63)

Continuing educators have realized for many years that, for what is now described as PCET to be effective, there has to be symbiosis between academic knowledge and the lived experience of the real, social world. As long ago as 1965 Edward Thompson delivered a typically trenchant lecture on this theme of 'Education and Experience' (Thompson, 1965). As with many other aspects of the culture of continuing education, the centrality of this integration between education and experience has now been recognized, belatedly, by at least the more progressive elements in the mainstream system. Once this seemingly obvious concept is acknowledged, a number of radical changes to the system (should) become inevitable. Most obviously, curriculum approaches in education generally, but in the disciplinary-bound world of HE in particular, must become more flexible, more interdisciplinary and more responsive to the social, as well as economic, demands of the wider society. 'It brings centrally into consideration "the reflective practitioner" in all walks of life: the active citizen (see below); participatory workplace and other democracy; "tacit knowledge"' (Duke, 1997, p. 66). It also brings centre stage the whole complex of APEL, credit transfer and CATS.

This of course carries social and educational dangers, as well as benefits. Quality and standards could be threatened by giving undue regard to non-educational factors; and instrumental vocationalism could come to dominate both FE and HE policy. Neither of these outcomes is however, inevitable.

Flexible, sensitive but rigorous and comprehensive quality assurance (QA) procedures for both FE and HE are major requirements for a successful lifelong learning system. Of course, this must incorporate non-standard HE as well as the mainstream of full-time and part-time degrees: CVE/CPD, individual credit bearing modules, and the plethora of vocational credit and award-bearing schemes, all need to be included in a comprehensive QA framework. An enormous amount of learning in contemporary society occurs outside the formal framework altogether. Cropley has drawn attention to 'the educative role of the workplace, zoos, museums, libraries, clubs, churches, political parties and similar organizations. Even recreational activities . . . can be seen as having a significant educational value' (Knapper and Cropley, 1991, p. 35). A new flexibility needs to emerge which recognizes and values such learning and integrates it with more established, formal patterns of learning. APEL systems, now beginning to cope satisfactorily with the appropriate accreditation of formal education and training, have to confront the much more difficult issue of accrediting experiential learning. This needs, however, to be a genuinely integrative model of flexible learning, with appropriate QA mechanisms — not based on the assumption that all non-formal learning must be deconstructed and then redefined in terms of the existing FE and HE norms.

Two final aspects of general social change should be noted: the position of women in society, and the greater acceptance of multiculturalism. It remains true that universities, in terms of their academic and academic-related staff, are heavily dominated by men, particularly at senior levels. The feminization of higher education and its culture has a long way to go — as a cursory look around any Senate or Academic Board meeting will confirm. Nevertheless, in terms of the student body in FE and HE, but particularly the latter, the change in gender balance since the mass expansion of PCET has been striking. Middle-class young women as a proportion of the student body have increased markedly. In the traditional universities, while there has been an increase between 1980–81 and 1990–91 of 9 per cent in male enrolments in full-time courses, and 37 per cent in part-time courses, for female enrolments the corresponding figures were 40 per cent and 76 per cent. In the new universities, the pattern is even more pronounced. The increase in male enrolments for full-time was 50 per cent and for part-time 10 per cent; the corresponding figures for the increase in female enrolments were 85 per cent for full-time and 143 per cent for part-time (NCE, 1993, p. 293). Similarly, changing employment patterns, and changes in family structure, with far more single, working mothers, have encouraged the growth of education and training for women in their twenties to late thirties. And this whole development has been in part cause and in part effect of the wider women's liberation movement of the 1970s and 1980s.

Whereas there is some discernible difference in gender balance in the student body between the traditional universities and the new, particularly in the number of part-time female students, there is a much sharper divergence in the proportion of students from the ethnic minority communities (as there is in terms of social class). This is explained in part by the fact that large numbers of ethnic minority students are part-time and local, thus making the new universities more attractive and appropriate; in part by the more vocationally oriented programmes of the new universities; and in part by their generally lower and more flexible entry requirements.

Higher Education and Social Criticism

Overall, therefore, a variety of social trends has increased the attractiveness and perceived relevance of higher education for a far larger proportion of the population than in the past. Many analyses of these social changes in contemporary society, which are broadly mirrored in other Western societies, go on to argue that the more heterogeneous, flexible and atomized nature of society should be viewed within the framework of post-modernism. How does the 'democratic imperative', which was alluded to at the beginning of this chapter, fit within this context? Post-modernism — which is discussed in more depth, in terms of its implications for the future of HE, in chapter 8 above — denies the validity of any absolute moral, political or normative values. Everything is relative, there are no universal laws, no 'meta-narratives', and certainly no place for ideological frameworks such as liberalism or socialism. One of the many glaring fallacies of post-modernism is, as Peter Osborne has noted, its failure to recognize that 'the narrative of the death of meta-narrative is itself grander than most of the narratives it would consign to oblivion' (Osborne in Eagleton, 1996, p. 34).

Higher education, in this climate of post-modernism, has multifaceted roles, but the traditional liberal framework is certainly challenged. A part of the post-modernist assault has been to deny the validity or even the possibility of academic objectivity (see, for example, Fieldhouse, 1985). '. . . The possibility of securing objective knowledge and of pursuing truth in a disinterested way can no longer be assumed' because of what Ron Barnett has termed the 'epistemological undermining' (Barnett, 1990, p. 189) of the bases of liberalism.

If the liberal basis of HE is thus under attack, how much more so is the social purpose perspective of continuing education. Yet this must be a key element of the Lifelong Learning University. A defining characteristic of lifelong learning has to be a concern with and commitment to the widest possible involvement of the adult population in PCET, in order to contribute to the development of a democratic, participative society and culture. This can be, and has been, articulated in a variety of liberal and socialist frameworks. However, they all have in common the *a priori* assertion of the need for a value framework.

Arguably, there are three main models within which the 'democratic imperative' to buttress active citizenship and participatory democracy can be pursued: the social cohesion, consensus model; the liberal, personal development model; and the radical, critical analytical model. As with most such schema, these are not in practice discrete and they have many overlapping characteristics. At the very least, though, they signal significant differences of emphasis.

The social cohesion model stems from a functionalist approach to social analysis. Thus, universities exist primarily to provide education and training, and cultural induction, which are conducive to the development of the prevailing social and economic system. On the assumption that the existing structure of market capitalism and the accompanying parliamentary democratic structures are the necessary and sufficient systemic foundation for our society, then universities should provide programmes and a wider culture which support such structures. At its crudest level, this can shade into instrumental vocationalism: the notion that, essentially, HE is there to provide uncritical, technological training which will ensure an appropriate supply of graduates to staff efficiently the institutions of market capitalism. More positively, though, such an ideological stance can accommodate a broader, more liberal approach which ensures the achievement not only of 'training' but of cultural integration into the assumptions and practices underlying what is seen as the prevailing pluralistic, parliamentary democratic system.

The second, mainstream liberal model emphasizes personal development as a major benefit deriving from the HE experience, not only for the individual concerned, but for the wider society. This has been particularly explicit within the adult education tradition but is implicit in the orthodox cultural stance of the old universities. Albert Mansbridge, the founder of the Workers Educational Association (WEA), believed strongly that the fundamental, *a priori*, justification for both university extension and the WEA was the acquisition of 'education for education's sake'. This was construed by Mansbridge, and with little change of substance by his successors, as being primarily about the acquisition by the mass of people of the joys of culture — in the sense of high culture. The subtext of this enthusiasm for literature, art, history, music and the arts as a whole was the induction of the newly enfranchised working class — or at least its opinion-forming sections — into the dominant culture. (For a trenchant critique as well as history of the WEA, see Fieldhouse, 1978.) Whilst this motivation has remained conceptually intact, as the twentieth century progressed so the emphasis in practice has been much more upon the provision of culturally-oriented adult education for the already well-educated middle class. (For a discussion of these issues see Thompson, 1980; Taylor, 1996.)

This tradition has also, however, had a concern with critical, open thinking, and with responsiveness to student opinion — on curriculum, on the substantive issues under discussion and upon the interaction of life experience and academic knowledge (see Taylor et al., 1985, 1996).

The personal development model has underlain much of the orthodox culture of the overall university system — though without the emphasis so evident in adult education and lifelong learning upon student participation and the need for symbiosis between education and experience. This has to be qualified in two obvious senses. The liberal model, as briefly sketched here, applied to the arts and social science areas, and to an extent to the pure sciences, but it has never had much purchase upon the applied science, technology, and vocational areas, such as engineering, medicine, business studies et al. Secondly, the Thatcherite onslaught on all aspects of liberalism through the 1980s certainly had a profound impact upon HE. The liberal model, though it has survived, has been battered and breached in a whole variety of ways, both practical and ideological.

Nevertheless, there are obvious connections here with the radical, critical model. In this context, too, the history of adult and continuing education provides a clear microcosm of the more amorphous debates in the wider, mainstream system. From the early days of university extension in the 1870s (see Jepson, 1973), and particularly in the early years of the twentieth century when the WEA was developing (see Fieldhouse, 1978), there was a strong socialist current which saw the main purpose and function of the movement as being the education and radicalizing of key sections of the industrial working class. Advocates of this perspective ranged from those who espoused a Labourist, or social democratic, reformist view through to Marxists of various hues. For the former, adult education was seen as a key means of equipping the working class to obtain and then exercise power in a responsible and informed way. The most important subjects here were therefore politics, history, economics, sociology and industrial relations — and the key student groups, trade unionists and other working-class activists. Such educational experience would provide the Labour Movement with the personnel to achieve the process of radical reform, but through the established constitutional and ideological structures (see Miliband, 1972). This continued the radical reform tradition with its emphasis upon the importance of education, which stretches back at least to the Chartists and arguably well before that (see Thompson, 1963). Generally, this model has assumed that contemporary society not only should be but can be reformed through rational argument, within the context of an educational and informed electorate, using the existing social and political institutions. It has thus been closely allied not only to the Labour Movement but to the ideology of 'Labourism' (see Miliband, 1972; Coates, 1975).

The contemporary context of HE — and of continuing education — has changed significantly since the heyday of this type of workers' education. Nevertheless, as noted earlier, both the pedagogic experience of CE in teaching working-class employees, and the innovative curriculum developed, are centrally relevant to the lifelong learning concept.

The minority, but important, Marxist elements in the social purpose tradition generally reflected the revolutionary politics of the far Left, believing in explicitly socialist (usually Marxist) education as a key element in either or both of cadre or rank-and-file political education. The primary body here was the National Council of Labour Colleges, established to promote Marxist-oriented working-class education to counter the bourgeois, liberal education of the Workers Educational Association (WEA) (Fieldhouse, 1996, Chapter 7; Millar, 1979).

This radical Marxist view of education had a profound influence on community education — as discussed in chapter 15 — and has been a consistent element in university continuing education. However, as Roger Fieldhouse and others have argued, the best Marxist education is by definition critical, analytical and rigorous, rather than dogmatic, closed and rigid, in its approach. There is thus a close connection between this social purpose CE and the liberal view of education in general, and lifelong learning in particular.

For a variety of reasons, many of them discussed earlier in this and the preceding chapter, the liberal approach to education has come under considerable attack in the past 15 years, from both the left and the right — but especially

the latter (see Taylor, 1996). However, for the development of a lifelong learning system which connects with the social trends indicated here, and rearticulates the essential purposes of higher education in that new context, it is clear that a revitalized liberal approach is essential. But how should this be defined? Each of the models presented schematically here is sharply distinct: and yet, as indicated, there are substantial connections and overlapping ideological themes. The appropriate culture and approach of the Lifelong Learning University is inherently pluralist: thus it may be that no single, simple model of liberalism is appropriate. Rather, the basis for development in response to the complex of social, contextual issues outlined may be the spectrum of approaches noted. The democratic imperative requires both functional involvement and personal development perspectives: even more, it requires a radical, critical educational programme and the involvement of large numbers of individuals and key sectional groups in the community.

Responding to Dearing

The Dearing Report also refers frequently, but usually briefly and often allusively, to the role of higher education in cultural production and personal development. Nevertheless, its heart is in the right place, as in the following section of the Summary Report:

> As the world becomes ever more complex and fast-changing, the role of higher education as a guardian or transmitter of culture and citizenship needs to be protected. Higher education needs to help individuals and society to understand and adapt to the implications of change, while maintaining the values which make for a civilized society. (NCIHE, 1997, Summary Report, p. 12)

19 Lifelong Learning and the University Community

To make anything of the Dearing recommendations in a practical way, the internal community (and culture) of the university will have to respond positively and to adapt. In crude management-speak this is often referred to as 'changing the culture', but what is interesting about the Dearing Report (and is echoed in much of our personal analysis of its implications) is how far Dearing also wants to see aspects of 'traditional' university culture restored and enhanced as well as acceptance of innovation and change.

As has been argued throughout this book, to be effective the new mass system of higher education has to be characterized by the lifelong learning perspective. Indeed, the Dearing Committee Report makes lifelong learning the main organizing concept of its analysis. In the very first paragraph of the Report is the claim that in the twenty-first century society should become 'committed, through effective education and training, to lifelong learning' (NCIHE, 1997, Main Report 1.1).

What will these changes entail for British universities, in terms of their internal culture and practices? It should be noted first that, profound though the change to a mass system undoubtedly is, the emerging structure will obviously evolve from the existing institutional complex. The university system will continue to be characterized by diversity and by primary commitments to research and teaching and learning, though probably with significantly greater emphasis upon the latter. The institutional spectrum will certainly persist and there is likely to be at least as much hierarchical distinction as now between those universities perceived as the elite and the rest. No committee of inquiry could have changed these and related cultural and structural features of the system. A fundamental radicalization of the system would require committed and interventionist government action, and, despite its rhetoric and its no doubt many admirable qualities, the new Labour government shows no immediate signs of moving in this direction.

With these conservative caveats, what then is the nature of the changes that can be envisaged? In broad cultural terms, the elite university system existed essentially to ensure the reproduction of the elite stratum for successive generations. This entailed inducting the elite of each generation into the liberal education and awareness necessary for the governing or ruling groups in society, including an appreciation of high culture, the historical evolution of (Western) society, and the mainsprings of the current organizational structures of society and the rationales underpinning them. The system also included, crucially, high

quality vocational training for key professions. Whilst there have been huge changes in both these sets of functions reflecting broader socioeconomic change, there has also been considerable continuity. Thus, for example, the strong and unbroken traditions of the English literary canon and a commitment to the British parliamentary system and wider constitutional arrangements, have remained central concerns for the universities. Similarly, there has been a continuing concern with professional training in the well-established professions, such as law and medicine (though the universities' original and primary concern with the training of civil servants and the clergy has of course declined markedly).

It goes without saying that these central functions have been extended, modified and in some ways transformed through the twentieth century and particularly since the 1960s. Since the ending of the binary division in 1992 the whole HE system has become both more pluralistic in its provision and more diverse in its institutional missions. Over the next decade these trends will become more pronounced. In terms of their teaching and learning functions, few if any institutions will be able, or wish, to rely exclusively on traditional background students, registered on conventional three-year full-time degree programmes. The HE system as a whole will develop far greater contact and cooperation with the outside world. Again, it should be stressed that such contact and cooperation exists already in many areas — engineering, social work, medicine, and business studies, for example. But, as Dearing recommends, such contact and cooperation needs to be extended so that ideally all, or nearly all, students have a year of relevant work experience built into their curriculum design. Such partnership arrangements will clearly have financial and organizational dimensions which will need to be clarified.

Stake-holders

Employers are clearly key partners in this process. The common assumption, however, that this means largely if not exclusively private sector employers needs to be challenged. Also, there is much more to the outside world than employers, however broadly defined. Universities need to interact with their whole communities, in the ways described earlier in chapter 15. It is all too typical of contemporary thinking that the outside world is assumed to be a *declassé*, homogeneous, and in economic terms oriented exclusively to the so-called free market. This is almost always implicit rather than explicit — once stated, its oversimplification and ideological bias are apparent. In the aftermath of the Dearing Report it will be important to emphasize these points, not least in discussion with the government. CE specialists have a key bridging role here, given their extensive contacts and partnership arrangements with a range of agencies and organizations in the wider community.

Linked to this theme, and to the Dearing Report's emphasis upon the need for increased attention to quality in learning and teaching, is the change

in the teaching function in universities away from the transmission of disciplinary knowledge to the facilitation of learning (as discussed in chapter 8).

Closely linked to these concerns over curriculum development is the need to empower the student, another theme prominent in the Dearing Report. There are of course financial dimensions to this — as is the suggestion (discussed in chapter 13) that public funding should follow the student. The premise is a more pronounced shift to demand-led, student-oriented provision.

It should be noted that this too is fraught with problems of both principle and practice. How far should national needs, as perceived by government, employers and others, be key determinants of provision? How are quality criteria and demand-led provision to be reconciled? To what extent should established academic disciplines and methodologies be allowed to determine curriculum content, and assessment?

There are also other dimensions to curriculum change, which are connected more to the democratization of higher education. Within adult and continuing education there has been a long-established practice of curriculum and syllabus negotiation and partnership between academic staff (and the university and its procedures) and the student body. On occasion, as with the provision of industrial studies for trade unionists, a third partner organization has been involved in curriculum discussions (see Taylor, 1997). At its best, this tradition has embodied a symbiosis between education and experience, between the academic epistemology of the university and the real world concerns, experiences and perceptions of the (adult) student body.

Such negotiated practice can be difficult. The context of mainstream, credit and award-bearing HE is both different and more complex than the world of adult and continuing education. How, precisely, this practice can be built into the new mass system will require detailed consideration and will be inherently contentious; but there can be no doubt that, in a system characterized by the facilitation of learning, rather than the transmission of knowledge, and by a genuine partnership between students, universities and the outside world and its agencies, the attempt has to be made.

A further change necessary in the new system is the need to acknowledge the heterogeneity of the student body and its needs. Academic staff need to become equally at ease with CPD, post-experience students, mature part-time and full-time degree students, CE students enrolled on discrete credit-bearing modules, as well as with the conventional full-time degree and standard age and background students. Such adjustment is in part psychological, but it is also substantively a realization that the pedagogy for the new system needs to take full recognition of experiential factors as well as academic, disciplinary-based knowledge. This is easy to state but profoundly difficult to put into practice. What precisely does this entail? How is a correct balance, and accommodation, to be reached between appropriate academic and methodological rigour, and the insistent demands of practicality, experience and the varying perspectives of the outside world? How is high quality to be maintained, and

indeed defined, in the new context? How far is inter-disciplinarity compatible with the maintenance of high quality? These and other related questions have yet to be addressed in any depth by the universities. It may be, also, that very different responses will be appropriate in the different disciplinary areas.

Social Purpose

Perhaps the most difficult and contentious area of cultural change is that of cultural transmission and social purpose. According to Sir Ron Dearing, his Committee paid particular attention to the appropriate response to Robbins' fourth principle, 'transmitting a common culture and common standards of citizenship'. Dearing's formulation, in his Report, and as highlighted in an article in the *Times Higher Education Supplement*, is the admonition to higher education to be part of the conscience of a democratic society, founded on respect for the rights of the individual and the reciprocal responsibilities of the individual to society as a whole (Dearing, 1997; NCIHE, 1997, p. 8).

This is unexceptionable to all but the most hard-line of neo-liberal individualists, but it side-steps critically important social and political questions for institutions. As Robbins argued, universities have as one of their functions the transmission of a common culture. In effect, this means liberal culture. The complicating factor noted by Dearing — that this common culture is now complex and multicultural rather than monolithic (which was anyway a notably false assumption even in the 1960s) — is of critical importance but confirms and prioritizes rather than negates HE's role in this context. Exactly how this role is defined and articulated is one of the major challenges to face universities over the next decade. Difficult though it is, the potential emergence of a new mass system, characterized by flexibility of curriculum and pedagogy, and by a heterogeneous student body, provides the context to make this both an essential and an achievable element in the new HE system.

A related issue, and one that has been at the heart of adult and continuing education, is that of 'social purpose'. The liberal tradition in HE generally, and CE in particular, has many facets (Taylor et al., 1985), including an emphasis upon personal development and education as an *a priori* goal. But it has also, and crucially, embodied a commitment to education as a means of collective social change, as was discussed in chapter 18. The Dearing Report gives considerable prominence to the need to widen participation and to increase accessibility to universities. The implicit rationales for this commitment are to increase economic efficiency and to create a fairer society, in terms of greater equality of opportunity for individual citizens. However, social purpose, even within the mildly reformist social democratic tradition, is about much more than such liberal, individualistic perspectives. Education, and particularly HE, has been seen as a key agency for emancipating, informing and empowering the disadvantaged.

If the commitment in the new system to democratization is to be more than rhetorical it has to embody both the more democratic structures and processes within HE itself, as described in this chapter, and an ideological commitment to seeing universities, and post-compulsory education as a whole, as key agencies in developing a more egalitarian, participatory, and socially just — in short a more democratic — society. This of course offends against post-modern conceptions of the relativism, amorality and essential conservatism of society generally, including the education system. And, at least as expressed in these terms, it is perhaps unlikely to find favour with a New Labour government.

These are then difficult issues, conceptually, organizationally and politically. The context for their discussion and, optimistically, resolution has been created by the Dearing Report but this provides only the context and thus the beginning for the necessary discussions and policy formulation and implementation.

If these are the main cultural issues for the new system, what are the practical concerns in managing organizational change to facilitate the new mass system? Naturally, these practical issues mirror the broader cultural issues discussed above. In terms of overall structure, the first tasks are to construct mechanisms for widening participation, to develop curriculum appropriately and to build partnerships with outside agencies, as indicated earlier. This in turn requires that the teaching and learning roles of the university are given equal status and priority, to research activity — and that they are funded adequately. Crucially, as Dearing recognizes, there must be underpinning support for the scholarship necessary to deliver high quality teaching and learning. The traditional primacy given to the 'leading' research universities — and the correspondingly lower status accorded to many of the predominantly teaching institutions will need to be questioned. Intimately linked to this is the need for the universities to review methods and modes of teaching and learning, within a quality assured framework. With a more heterogeneous student body, with varied academic backgrounds and qualifications and often with considerable life and work experience, pedagogic approaches and curriculum content will need fundamental review. Thus for cultural and sociological reasons, as much as for the pressing economic arguments, traditional methods of teaching within the university system will need to change. One key aspect of the transition to this new way of working is the construction of a more widely respected and utilized credit-rated system.

The Dearing Report endorses, but neither emphasizes nor makes practical recommendations about, the desirability of instituting a National Credit Framework (NCF) (NCIHE, 1997, Main Report, Chapter 10). For a fully-fledged lifelong learning system to operate, such a national framework is of course essential, as David Robertson pointed out in *Choosing to Change* (Robertson, 1994). A flexible system, with students stepping in and stepping out, and requiring credit and/or CPD provision through their adult lives, depends upon ease of transfer and the counting of credit across the HE system. This is particularly the case given that occupational and geographical mobility is increasing so markedly, especially among the graduate population.

The first step is for such a system to be agreed nationally. At the same time, regional credit frameworks (incorporating whenever possible FE as well as HE institutions and credit) need to be developed further. All this is difficult enough but the crucial elements to make any such framework practicable and operative on a large scale are, firstly, that there should be a closer 'fit' between curricula in the degree schemes and other programmes provided by universities; and, secondly, that there should be both the perception and the reality of explicit and agreed standards across all HE levels and across all HE institutions. The Dearing Report's recommendations on the national framework of qualifications, and on the roles for the new Quality Assurance Agency, are of fundamental importance and provide the basis for beginning to move towards the objectives noted. However, real progress will depend upon political will, funding embodying incentives for change and, not least, a sense of urgency on the part of universities' senior and middle management.

For such a credit framework to operate effectively a nationally coordinated and universally applied quality assurance system is essential. In addition to this an ethos of collaboration and partnership, rather than competition, needs to be established. This, as Kennedy noted in relation to FE (Kennedy, 1997), is a major cultural and political change after the 18 years of Conservative government dedicated to instilling a thoroughgoing market mentality into education, as everything else. To establish such partnerships and to enable the transfer of student credit and the congruence of provision between institutions will not be easy. It cannot be achieved by university management alone (still less by government); it is essentially a professional challenge and requires specialists from the broad disciplinary areas to work together across institutional (and often sectoral) boundaries to establish academically coherent, cost effective and high quality programmes.

In practical terms, one of the most important areas for development is distance learning making full use of modern technology. A mass, modularized HE system based on credit systems and flexibility will depend increasingly upon home-based and work-based study via electronic communication. There are obvious financial savings to be made here, especially when such IT-based provision becomes large scale. However, not only will there be significant capital investment costs, there are also staff development needs and careful planning required to ensure that quality is assured through an appropriate mix of distance and face-to-face learning.

Responding to Dearing

What then, in summary, lies at the heart of the institutional change in HE resulting from the prospects of a mass system? Tentatively, we would suggest three key requirements. First, there should be a commitment to flexibility of provision, geared towards both student demand and the perceived needs of society, within a quality-assured framework. Secondly, and closely related to this is the need for substantial curriculum development and the accompanying staff development required. Thirdly, at a rather different level, the new system should be based centrally upon a commitment to democratization, in the ways we have described, and embodying a revitalized liberal approach to the purposes and practices of HE.

Part 6

Postscript

20 The Dearing Vision: A Prognosis

The Vision

Much has been made in the immediate aftermath of the publication of the Dearing Report of its size, scope and ambition: the 1700 pages of text; the weight of the boxed set (6.5 kg); the volume of paper on its way to the Record Office (including nearly 1000 official submissions and records of evidence); and above all the 93 recommendations (nearly all in multiple clauses). In these circumstances it is importance to capture the essence of the Report and its vision, and to try to separate out the big, or overarching ideas.

The vision encompasses an explicit attempt to preserve, but also to up-date the Robbins legacy. Dearing is, however, especially concerned to embed higher education within a wider set of social purposes: 'central to our vision is a judgment that the United Kingdom will need to develop as a learning society' (NCIHE, 1997, Main Report 1.1). This leads on to reworking of Robbins' four main aims and objectives for higher education ('instruction in skills for employment', 'promoting the general powers of the mind', 'advancing learning', and 'transmitting a common culture and common standards of citizenship') (ibid., Main Report 5.7). Dearing's 'four main purposes' are set out in figure 20.1.

We suggest that there are four 'big' ideas which underpin this vision in practical terms:

1   *The contribution of higher education to lifelong learning,* as embedded particularly in the qualifications framework, views on articulation and collaboration between education sectors, and especially fairer and more effective support for all types of learners in HE.
2   *A vision for learning in the twenty-first century,* as embodied in ideas about credit and the qualifications framework (again), assurance of standards as well as quality, teacher professionalism, communication and information technology, key skills, and work experience.
3   *Funding research according to its intended outcomes,* as set out in the multi-stranded model for research evaluation and funding. The Report makes a brave attempt to cut through the rather sterile and tactical controversy over concentration and dispersal of research funding, hyped while the Committee was at work by the immediate aftermath of the 1996 RAE.
4   *A new compact between the state, the institutions and their students,* involving especially a 'deal' whereby institutions retain their independence and gain increased security in return for clearer accountability

(especially on standards) and greater responsiveness to a wide range of legitimate stake-holders. Governance and collaboration are also relevant here, as is the notion that a greater student contribution to costs is matched by assured outcomes.

Figure 20.1   The Dearing 'purposes' of higher education

- to inspire and enable individuals to develop their capabilities to the highest potential levels throughout life, so that they grow intellectually, are well-equipped for work, can contribute effectively to society and achieve personal fulfilment;

- to increase knowledge and understanding for their own sake and to foster their application to the benefit of the economy and society;

- to serve the needs of an adaptable, sustainable, knowledge-based economy at local, regional and national levels;

- to play a major role in shaping a democratic, civilized, inclusive society.

Source: NCIHE, 1997, Main Report 5.11.

What is more, none of these ideas (or those which accompany them) stands alone. As the Report concludes: '[o]ur recommendations add up to a coherent package for higher education. We do not intend that those to whom they are addressed should choose to implement only some of them. The new compact requires commitment from all sides' (NCIHE, 1997, Main Report 24.1). We offer our own evaluation of the compact, from the perspectives of lifelong learning and the university in the next chapter.

Dearing and New Labour

In responding immediately to the Report on 23 July 1997, the new Secretary of State echoed the language of the compact, announcing what he described as 'a new deal for higher education — addressing the universities' funding problems; protecting free higher education for the less well off; ensuring that no parent has to pay up front contributions; and offering a fair deal for students and graduates' (Blunkett, 1997). He thus courageously grasped the nettle of funding reform from student contributions and exorcized the ghost of Keith Joseph a decade and a half earlier.

However, it quickly became clear that the government's own proposals for student contributions and support, not based on any of the models painstakingly analysed by Dearing, had not at the time been fully thought through (see chapter 12 above) (DfEE, 1997b). They sprang an instant response, with concerns over students who had already or intended to negotiate a 'gap' year, as well as pressure on the Clearing system of qualified students anxious to get in to the system before the free tuition boom was lowered. Such uncertainties were also compounded by controversy over how much 'new' money might

Figure 20.2   DfEE 'extra' funding: 1998–99

- £125m for institutions
      approx £65m to reduce 'efficiency gains'
      approx £60m for backlog in maintenance and equipment

- £36m for student support
      £22m for access funds
      £10m to support graduates taking up teaching
      £4m for £250 hardship loans (approx 16,000 students)

- £4m to lift the cap on HEFCE 'sub-degree numbers' in FE (approx 1000 places)

- Total £165m

Source: CVCP, 1997c.

actually end up with institutions in order to purchase education of the quality the contributing students deserve. Ministers were initially reduced simply to stating their intentions to press the case in the November 1997 public expenditure round.

The logjam appeared to break at the Labour Party conference in Brighton in September 1997. In an unusual departure from budget-setting convention, the Secretary of State for Education and Employment announced an injection of an extra £165m into higher education in England in the 1998–99 financial year, the year in which the government's means-tested fee is due to be introduced. Analysis by the CVCP of the likely effects is set out in figure 20.2.

Notwithstanding the political context of this announcement (in the arena in which the first organized challenge to graduate contributions might have been expected to appear — in fact , it did not) and of the similar announcements by the Prime Minister anticipating an extra 500,000 students in higher education by the end of the life of the Parliament, these are significant steps towards meeting Dearing's short-term funding needs (estimated at £350m for the 1998–99 financial year). The key remaining gap is on the capital side. David Blunkett also clarified the starting point for repayment of loans as an income (for 1998 graduates) of £10,000.

The medium term-prognosis for new Labour and HE is, however, still uncertain. We can, at this stage point to the following promising signs, in addition to the funding steps set out above:

1   the pre-election and manifesto commitments to an integrating philosophy of lifelong learning, plus the intention to use this term in the title of an early White Paper on Further and Higher Education (Labour Party, 1996);

2   the immediate, positive response to the Dearing recommendations on funding (although by not choosing any recognizable variant on the models chosen by Dearing, the government could be said to have lost an opportunity);

3   the role of advanced training (F *and* HE) in meeting the government's central first term target of reducing youth unemployment;
4   the early initiatives along the lines of Individual Learning Accounts and a Learning Bank; and
5   the commitment to regional development.

Dearing and the CVCP

Meanwhile, other parties to the political compact have been signifying their willingness to play. The CVCP, at their residential conference in Strathclyde in September 1997, apparently swallowed large parts of the developmental agenda suggested by Dearing for the sector, including critically the strictures on quality, standards and qualifications. Unresolved issues included a muted opposition to the 'scholarship' stream of research funding and severe doubts about the F/HE boundary, but Chairman Martin Harris caught the mood well with his closing speech:

> Today, I want to announce CVCP's new partnership with students. As a signal of our intent to honour our side of the Dearing compact, CVCP is making a set of clear commitments for the millennium. These commitments — this new partnership with students — will secure and deliver the education that students should expect and which will equip them for work and life in the twenty-first century.
>
> I now want to outline some of the details of the new partnership. It is built upon three main themes:
>
> - first, enhanced access to higher education
> - second, high quality education for students
> - third, guaranteed standards which employers and students alike want to see.
>
> To take access first, we see two key elements in the new partnership resumed expansion and widening participation. Given the political will to deliver adequate resources, we can make both of these aspirations a reality. (CVCP, 1997d)

The University: 'Rhetoric and Reality'

One of the main effects of the composite Dearing recommendations is to take seriously the university system's claimed commitments to a number of strategic objectives: flexibility of curricular response; mutual assurance of standards; equality of opportunity in admissions and employment; innovation in teaching and learning; and mature academic democracy. Our analysis of the current academy has called into question aspects of each of these elements. In each case there is evidence of the rhetoric outweighing the reality: the 'phantom modular courses', the resistance to external peer review, the conservatism of admissions decisions, the serious lack of fit between the demography of the student body (on gender, ethnicity and disability) and the teaching staff; the priority afforded research over teaching, and the reluctance of academic governance to break free of the past.

Equally, we have expressed scepticism about the untrammelled market philosophy of higher education and brittle calls for 'changes of culture'. We believe that Dearing is right to express confidence in many of the achievements of UK higher education, not least the disciplined diversity of institutions which it now incorporates. But, just as bold steps are required by government, employers and students and their sponsors, we do need the university system to adapt, and to turn some of its more rhetorical commitments into reality if it is fully to play a part within the evolving world of lifelong learning. For it to do so will require an almost unprecedented exercise of collective will, as we believe we have demonstrated in our analysis of the Dearing recommendations and the current state of the university. Our ultimate conclusions are, however, broadly optimistic. With support as well as pressure from outside, the academy has adapted in the past, and it can do so again.

21   Lifelong Learning and UACE

The Universities Association for Continuing Education (UACE) represents at institutional level the interests of CE and its students across the whole HE sector. CE is defined, interpreted and articulated very differently according to institutional cultures and contexts. Nevertheless, CE's major focuses of concern are uniform: all aspects of HE provision for part-time mature students at both undergraduate and postgraduate levels, including some non-credit bearing provision. CE is characterized by its commitment to student-centred learning with an emphasis upon the fostering of critical, reflective thinking. In terms of 'types' of provision, CE encompasses continuing vocational education (including CPD and work-based learning), liberal adult education for personal development, and 'social purpose' CE (including developmental work with groups currently under-represented in HE).

In the lead-up to the writing of the Dearing Committee's Report UACE submitted a detailed paper, as part of the consultation exercise, which laid out UACE's proposals for the development of the HE system. The purpose of this section is to discuss how far the conclusions of the Dearing Report reflected these specific proposals, and the overall orientation of UACE.

The score-sheet of recommendations taken up from the UACE submission into the Dearing Report itself is a healthy one, and confirms the resonance of the Report's full title ('Higher Education *in the learning society*') from the perspective of the UK's most influential professional association concerned with continuing higher education.

There is much that UACE can welcome from the philosophical commitment to continuing education on a lifelong basis, the recognition of social and personal as well as economic purposes for higher education, and the prospects of more secure and rational funding streams, to acknowledgment of many of the practical items that have been on the UACE agenda for some time: credit; regional training and educational strategies; independent guidance; targeted staff development; and so on. Equally, there are other areas where we would have preferred Dearing to go the extra mile: on binding employers into the funding framework; on support for part-time and mixed-mode students; and on aspects of administrative reform such as a review (perhaps even the abolition) of the Teacher Training Agency.

The organizing concept of the Report is its commitment to lifelong learning. The very first paragraph states this commitment explicitly. CE, of course, is the key component of such an HE system, and its achievement would mark a fundamental change in the culture of British HE. In a lifelong learning system part-time, adult students, are the norm, returning throughout working life

— and indeed beyond — in order to update professional knowledge, learning for personal development and so on.

> People will need the knowledge and skills to control and manage their working lives. This requires a learning society, which embraces both education and training, for people at all levels of achievement, before, during and, for continued personal fulfilment, after working life. (NCIHE, 1997, Main Report 1.12–1.13)

There is also much support in the Report for greater accessibility, and for ensuring that the new mass system is characterized by the involvement of those groups in the community currently under-represented in HE. A whole chapter is devoted to widening participation and another to a wider analysis of the patterns of social and economic change, and the persistent patterns of inequality of opportunity and achievement, within HE structures.

The Report also places greater emphasis upon the need for developing a professional approach to pedagogy, curriculum and teaching, recognizing that new and more sophisticated approaches are needed in the light of both the increasing diversity of the student body, and the greater use of cost effective IT-based methods of delivery.

In all these ways, then, the Report's general orientation is very much in line with UACE's approach to the needs of the new, mass system: flexibility and diversity, within the context of assured quality, are seen as the keynotes.

At the broader ideological level there is perhaps more divergence between UACE's perspective and that of the Dearing Committee's Report. CE has had a long commitment to social purpose education (see Lovett, 1988; Fieldhouse, 1996; Ward and Taylor, 1986; Westwood and Thomas, 1991). Historically, this has been linked to both industrial studies work with trade unionists and more recently to community education with various disadvantaged groups (see chapters 15 and 18 above). Varied though this provision and the ideological commitments involved have been, there has been a consistent agenda of political radicalism. Underlying all such work has been a strong belief that its central purpose lay in its potential for contributing to radical social and political change. 'Knowledge is power' has been a key part of the CE creed. Times change, of course, and UACE's contemporary commitments are articulated in perhaps less overtly political tones. Nevertheless, the central concern with education, and particularly CE, as a means of achieving greater equality and, at least by implication, wider radical change has remained.

The Dearing Report, by contrast, sees increased accessibility and widened participation as justified essentially on two grounds. First, the Report argues that HE will need to respond to a predicted increase in demand. The rationale underlying this prediction is based upon 'the nature of the competitive environment' and the consequent need for a more skilled workforce; 'the economic benefits of participation in higher education to be gained for individuals and society'; the need to maintain high rates of participation at the 'traditional ages of entry, affected particularly by improving rates of achievement at Level 3';

and the increasing need for CPD and 'updating' provision (NCIHE, 1997, Main Report 6.43).

Secondly, it is assumed that the case for increased accessibility rests exclusively upon the *a priori* need for equality of opportunity, provided that quality can be maintained. '(The objective must be to reduce) the disparities in participation in higher education between groups and (to ensure) that higher education is responsive to the aspirations and distinctive abilities of individuals' (ibid., Main Report 7.1). Like the Robbins Committee of 1963, Dearing rejected the notion that 'more means worse': 'It is very often true that "people respond to opportunities that are available"' (ibid., Main Report 7.2).

All this is couched, not surprisingly for a government and therefore by definition an 'establishment' Committee, within a framework of liberal consensus. Liberal, pluralistic democracy is assumed to be not only the norm but to be desirable and, in effect, unchallenged. In as much as there is acknowledgment of inequalities of wealth and power, and the potential for social and political conflict, the role of HE is seen as palliative and conciliatory. This view is combined nicely, early in the Report, with a thoroughgoing individualism.

> Unless we address the under-representation of those from lower socioeconomic groups we may face increasingly socially divisive consequences. As a matter of equity, we need to reduce the under-representation of certain ethnic groups and of those with disabilities. Not least, there will be an increasing demand for higher education for its own sake by individuals seeking personal development, intellectual challenge, preparation for career change, or refreshment in later life. (ibid., Main Report 1.17)

These then are significant ideological differences of approach and long-term perspective. In the medium term policy context, however, there is a congruence: Dearing like UACE is wholly committed to lifelong learning, and thus CE broadly defined, as the central developmental aspect of the new HE system.

This congruence is not always translated, however, into the detail of the proposed changes as articulated through the Report's recommendations. UACE's proposals were grouped under four main headings: teaching and research; size, shape and structure; the wider contribution of HE to national life; and (inevitably) funding issues.

In terms of teaching and research, UACE had six main proposals. The first of these was for the establishment of a national credit framework for lifelong learning. To achieve this, UACE recommended that the principles for defining a uniformly accepted 'unit of credit' should be established by the Dearing Committee and that consideration should be given both to the operational objectives of the different parties concerned, and to the issue of whether such credit should apply to HE alone or should have a wider role. Further, the Committee should outline ways in which HEIs might be able to work with such a unit as a 'methodological instrument' within a changing framework of academic programmes.

The Report endorses the general principle of an NCF structure and usefully delineates a 'qualifications framework' (see figure 7.3 in chapter 7 above). It is argued powerfully that the establishment of such a framework would greatly facilitate trans-European CATS and would also help to standardize and quality assure the increasingly complex systems of awards within the UK. Dearing concludes that to achieve this entails both the acceptance of a 'national framework of qualifications' and 'placing a limit on the number of award titles' (ibid., Main Report 10.42). The Report goes on to identify the components of such a framework (ibid., Main Report 10.43–10.44). Recommendation 22 proposes that the framework outlined should be endorsed immediately by the government, representative bodies and the Quality Assurance Agency.

This certainly provides the basis for the development of an NCF structure which could become a key part of the new flexible step-in/step-out HE system. However, the central issue of how to ensure that HEIs actually use such a structure and enable CATS to operate for large numbers of students, is not discussed, let alone resolved. Unless and until HEIs can accept CATS procedures as a matter almost of routine, the NCF is in danger of remaining merely a bureaucratic structure with little purchase on the real world. Thus it would have been useful if Dearing could have taken up UACE's proposal to discuss ways in which institutions might be encouraged, or persuaded, to work with credit in this context. These are difficult issues, of course, as they involve not only congruence of curriculum and technical questions of compatibility of credit, but also more intangible but powerful perceptions of institutional reputation.

UACE's second concern in the area of teaching and research was to ensure that the new system should give greater recognition to the needs of the increasing mature student population. The Report certainly does acknowledge the growing proportion of mature students in HE both full-time and, particularly, part-time (ibid., Main Report 7.11–7.13). Further growth is predicted particularly in the area of CPD (ibid., Main Report 6.41): the Report notes, and agrees with, the CVCP view that the numbers of those with HE qualifications seeking to update their skills and knowledge 'could grow at a much faster rate as a consequence of the need for lifelong learning and continuing personal and professional development' (ibid., Main Report 6.41).

For UACE, however, perhaps the key issue was the achievement of a fully equitable system of funding for part-time students. This was not forthcoming from the Report and its recommendations (as is detailed in chapter 12). At a more general level, UACE was disappointed that the Report apparently confirmed the still prevalent view that the core of the HE student body, and the central reference point for teaching and learning programmes, is the three-year full-time undergraduate degree. The recommendations which address the need to improve the context of HE for part-time students are all indirect (for example, on the review of social security).

To put the point crudely, the Report implies that part-time students will have to continue to conform to the practices and structures of the full-time regime. The sole exception, as noted, is the Report's acknowledgment that CPD, on a self-funding basis and responsive to market demand, is very likely to grow.

UACE also advocated special attention being given to CE as a means of providing lifelong learning opportunities for those who have experienced educational disadvantage. As discussed earlier, the Report gives a high priority to widening participation and, albeit from a somewhat different ideological position, advocates the encouragement of greater accessibility for specific disadvantaged groups. In addition to funding issues, the Report has several recommendations which address these needs (see recommendations 2, 3, 4, 6, and 14 discussed in chapters 4, 12 and 13 above).

UACE emphasized in its submission the importance, within the teaching and learning context, of two further areas: CVE development, and IT and open learning methods of delivery. The commitment to CVE and its increasing importance in HE permeates the Report, as has already been noted. UACE welcomes this emphasis although the organization has concerns over the future of the dedicated HEFCE CVE funding, following the end of the current four-year planning period to 1998–99. If this funding, (totalling £61 million over the four years) were to be 'rolled up' in the formula based mainstream grant to HEIs there is the obvious danger that pump-priming involvement in CVE and CPD might disappear in at least some HEIs. (The current HEFCE evaluation project, based at the University of Birmingham, should be able to provide valuable guidance to HEFCE and HEIs on these issues in 1998.) On communications and information technology see our comments in chapter 8 above.

Finally, in this area, UACE stressed the importance of research in CE and lifelong learning within the emerging system. The Report does not address this issue, though implicitly its emphasis upon the need for professional training and development for teaching and learning, the priority given to QA, and the vision of a mass, flexible system, all point to the need for a rapid acceleration in research and development in post-compulsory education and training.

UACE's second group of proposals concerned the size, shape and structure of the system. Both UACE and the Report recognize the diversity of HEIs and welcome this as a strength within the new context. For example, the Report notes in its first chapter that 'Institutions of higher education . . . are and will be diverse . . . There should be no pressure on them to change their character' (ibid., Main Report 1.6). And again, in chapter 16 it is noted that

> such diversity has considerable strengths, especially in providing for student choice; in programme and pedagogic innovation; in the ability of institutions to capture the energy and commitment of staff; and in the ability of the sector as a whole to meet the wide range of expectations now relevant to higher education. Indeed, institutional diversity has been one of the important defining characteristics of the United Kingdom's higher education system and, with the concomitant flexibility and autonomy of mission afforded to institutions, is one of the features which distinguishes the UK from some of its international comparators. (ibid., Main Report 16.6)

The Report goes on to outline

two forces which we fear may be starting to affect adversely the proper diversity of provision. The first is the unintended pressure towards institutional homogeneity. The second is a latent danger of declining institutional self-discipline. (ibid., Main Report 16.10)

The consequent recommendation, with which UACE would concur, is 61 as discussed in chapter 16 above.

At a more general level of structure, UACE was concerned that the new system should facilitate participation by mature and part-time students. To the extent that the Report advocates, as already noted, both CVE/CPD and widened participation for disadvantaged groups, these concerns are amply reflected in the Report. However, there are real problems in relation to the funding proposals as they affect part-time and mature students, as is discussed below. Moreover, there is a worrying absence in the Report of the explicit recognition of CE students *per se*: that is, that very large numbers of adult students, particularly in traditional universities, who are registered on discrete credit-bearing modules rather than award-bearing programmes.

UACE welcomes the proposals for regional partnerships in the Report: and this is of course reflected in the Labour government's apparent enthusiasm for regional development more generally. The Report gives prominence to HEIs' regional roles.

In recent years, as we have suggested, there has been a growing emphasis on the local and regional role of higher education, to the extent that over three-quarters of institutions now refer to local and/or regional objectives in their strategic plans. At the same time there have been a number of attempts to measure the impact of higher education at local and regional level. (ibid., Main Report 12.8)

The Report goes on to detail the various ways in which HEIs contribute to the local and regional economy (ibid., Main Report, p. 191) and draws attention to the likely increase in adults engaging in HE study in their localities: '... not only will institutions provide, as they have historically done, programmes in the liberal arts and respond to leisure interests, but there will be an increasing opportunity and need for institutions to provide programmes that respond to specifically local social and economic needs for lifelong learning' (ibid., Main Report 12.26).

Emphasis is also given to the importance of local accessibility and to HEIs' roles in cultural and community development in their localities. A particular priority is given to the development of regional structures which link to EU developments, (ibid., Main Report 12.36) and to the needs of small and medium sized enterprises in HEIs' catchment areas (ibid., Main Report 12.48).

Recommendations 36 and 38, discussed in chapter 15, are concerned with these specific aspects of regional development.

What is not clear from the Report, however, is the way in which HEIs will be involved in the evolving regional bodies. In particular, there is no discussion of the complex questions of, first, national HE (and FE) funding structures in the context of regional bodies, and second, how exactly HEIs, with national and international missions, can relate to exclusively regional bodies. Finally, and most contentious of all, how can long-established traditions of institutional autonomy for HEIs be integrated within regional policy-making bodies?

At the outset of its Report, the Dearing Committee places some emphasis upon HE's wider contribution to national life, UACE's fourth area of proposals. In particular, Dearing advocates HE's role as 'part of the conscience of a democratic society, founded on respect for the rights of the individual and the responsibilities for the individual to society as a whole' and urges HE to 'sustain a culture which demands disciplined thinking, encourages curiosity, challenges existing ideas and generates new ones' (ibid., Main Report 1.4). These themes, and the associated liberal perspectives articulated in UACE's submission — for personal development and so on, find repeated expression throughout the Report. UACE's essentially liberal view of the nature of HE and its roles in the wider society are very similar to those found in the Report itself. The key issues, however, are how far these objectives can be realized in the real world context of the future, mass HE system, and to what extent the specific changes advocated by Dearing would facilitate such developments.

This leads directly to the last sub-area of UACE's submission, funding issues. This is the area of greatest contention nationally in the debate over Dearing: and it is one area where UACE's aspirations for its sector are clearly not met entirely by Dearing's recommendations. UACE emphasized the importance of resolving the longstanding injustice of the inequitable treatment of part-time students, and advocated a funded investigation into the feasibility of providing a financial incentive for HEIs to recruit learners from disadvantaged groups into HE. It also suggested, as did many others, a new funding system which incorporated both a 'graduate tax' and tax breaks for organizations and/ or for certain categories of individuals. Finally, UACE noted that economies of scale could be achieved through a mixed mode system using IT.

Some of these proposals are met by the Report. The last mentioned, on the developing use of IT, is a theme of the Report and several recommendations are devoted to this area. Recommendation 46 on student access to computers, in particular, is of key importance. However, it is unclear whether the recommendation (that all students will have access to a personal computer), refers to all students, part-time as well as full-time, postgraduate as well as undergraduate. Moreover, is it envisaged that this should apply only to students based in institutions, and registered on award-bearing programmes? It surely cannot be the intention — to take the extreme example — that all the hundreds of thousands of CE students registered on discrete credit-bearing modules off-campus should have such access. Similarly, some post-experience students on short intensive courses may well neither require nor be able to gain access to such equipment. There is a worrying absence here, as elsewhere in the Report, of a full recognition and understanding of the CE constituencies *per se*.

On the issue of encouraging accessibility the Report makes clear recommendations both that research should be undertaken on how best to encourage more participation for disadvantaged groups, and on how best to develop a system whereby more funding can be allocated to HEIs which enrol larger numbers of such students (see chapter 4 above). In addition, it is suggested that priority should be given in future to those HEIs which can demonstrate their strategic commitment to widening participation.

These are very considerable advances for the 'CE constituency' and they indicate clearly the ways in which, within the frameworks available, the funding councils might provide incentives for at least some HEIs to move towards a culture and practice which was more centred on accessibility and on the consequent need to develop curriculum and pedagogy appropriate to a more wide-ranging student body. Moreover, these recommendations are supported by detailed analysis and discussion, particularly in chapters 4 and 7, which provide the context and rationale for this policy stance.

However, on the key questions of proper financial provision for part-time students, the Report falls short of UACE's hopes and expectations.

UACE's particular concern is with the financial position of part-time adult students within the new system, rather than with the overall structure of student fees and, more generally, university finance. Nevertheless, at the most general level, there must be concern at the marked shift away from publicly financed HE provision whereby the state met most of the costs associated with undergraduate (full-time) study, to a system where the student or his or her family will be expected to pay the large bulk of both tuition fee and maintenance costs. There are many in UACE and elsewhere who would support as an *a priori* principle the AUT's view that 'education is a right not a privilege' and that therefore the costs of HE should be the responsibility of the state and should be met through taxation. However, in the real world it could be argued that some financial restructuring was essential: a mass system could not continue to be financed on the same fairly generous basis as the elite system had been. UACE's central concern therefore has to be two-fold: whether or not the new system advocated by Dearing (and subsequently amended significantly by the government) will have a seriously adverse effect on the recruitment of students from disadvantaged backgrounds into the HE system as a whole; and, secondly, and more specifically, what effects the new system will have upon CE students — that is, the whole range of part-time adult students registered on credit at whatever HE level.

On the first of these counts the Report makes some very positive statements and recommendations. It is stated, as a principle, that the new financial system should support as far as possible 'lifelong learning by making the choices between full and part-time, and between continuous and discontinuous study financially neutral; and reducing the disparity between support for students at further and higher education levels' (ibid., Main Report 20.2).

There follows an explicit statement that part-time students who are in receipt of benefit must not be deterred from entering higher education because they cannot afford the fees. To achieve this the Report concludes that the 'most appropriate approach would be a scheme where the funding bodies provide funding to allow institutions to remit fees for certain students. We estimate that the cost in 1998/99 would be some £15 million, and that the long-term cost would be some £50 million a year' (ibid., Main Report 20.9). It also suggests that eligibility for the Access Fund should be extended to part-time students. The full relevant recommendation is 76, discussed in chapter 12 above.

The Report points out that only a very few part-time students are eligible for mandatory grants or student loans. It might also have been added that, because of severe constraints on LEA funding as a result of government policy, very few discretionary grant awards have been made in recent years to part-time students.

Despite all the problems of resource constraints, and the equally strong cultural resistance to moving away from the 'gold standard' of the three-year full-time honours degree, UACE had hoped that full equity would be recommended for part-time students. The Report rejects this explicitly as is stated in the following paragraph

> We have considered whether loan or grant arrangements for supporting full-time students' living costs might be extended to part-time students but have concluded that there is a high proportion of part-time students who are in employment and therefore able to support themselves. Moreover it would be extremely expensive. Given the other requirements for additional funding which we have identified, we do not believe that this should be a priority call on any additional funding for higher education. We are concerned, however, that the current social security benefit rules are acting as a disincentive to part-time study for those who might reasonably be assumed to have the most to gain: those who are unemployed. (ibid., Main Report 20.11)

This is a considerable blow to the CE community. If adult students, including those registered on discrete credit-bearing modules rather than award-bearing programmes, are to be encouraged into HE they must have access to the full range of financial support available to full-time students. Under the system envisaged there is a danger that all part-time adult students (save those on benefit) will have the worst of all worlds: a harsher financial regime in HE generally, and the added penalty of their being debarred from its 'palliative' features.

Overall, then, the Dearing Report stops short of the full vision set out by UACE. Undoubtedly, the overall orientation to lifelong learning underlines the growing importance of CE and its student constituencies. Many of the specific recommendations if implemented would facilitate such development, as has been discussed. However, there remain both 'gaps' of important detail in the development envisaged, and several key explicit deficiencies. The continuing debate over the government's White Paper on Lifelong Learning and the subsequent legislation will provide the opportunity for UACE and others to press for the resolution of these problems. As with other Dearing reports (on the National Curriculum and 16–19 qualifications) the professional community hopes that those with responsibility for such actions are prepared to take the extra step for which the Report has so comprehensively cleared the ground.

References

ADONIS, A. (1997) 'Class apartheid', *Times Higher Education Supplement*, 10 October, p. 20.

AMIS, K. (1960) 'Lone voices — views of the fifties', *Encounter*, July, p. 9.

ANDERSON, P. (1965) 'Origins of the present crisis', in ANDERSON, P. and BLACKBURN, R. (eds) *Towards Socialism*, published for the New Left Review, London: Fontana.

BALL, C. (1990) Royal Society of Arts *More Means Different: Widening Access to Higher Education*, London: RSA.

BARNETT, R. (1990) *The Idea of Higher Education*, Milton Keynes: SRHE and Open University Press.

BARNETT, R. (1994) *The Limits of Competence: Knowledge, Higher Education and Society*, Buckingham: SRHE and Open University Press.

BARNETT, R. (1997a) 'Beyond competence', in COFFIELD, F. and WILLIAMSON, B. (eds) *Repositioning Higher Education*, Buckingham: SRHE and Open University Press.

BARNETT, R. (1997b) *Higher Education: A Critical Business*, Buckingham: SRHE and Open University Press.

BIGGS, C. et al. (1994) Employment Department Group *Thematic Evaluation of Enterprise in Higher Education Initiative*, Research Strategy Branch, Sheffield: Employment Department.

BINES, H. and WATSON, D. (1992) *Developing Professional Education*, Buckingham: SRHE and the Open University Press.

BLUNKETT, D. (1997) 'Government responds to Dearing Committee report on higher education', Department for Education and Employment Press Release 226/97, 23 July.

BOCOCK, J. (1997) *Accreditation and Teaching in Higher Education*, Report for the Planning Group on Accreditation of Teaching in HE, September.

BOCOCK, J. and SCOTT, P. (1994) *Re-drawing the Boundaries: Further and Higher Education Partnerships*, Leeds: Centre for Policy Studies in Education, University of Leeds.

BOCOCK, J. and WATSON, D. (1994) (eds) *Managing the University Curriculum. Making Common Cause*, Buckingham: SRHE and Open University Press.

BOYER, E.L. (1990) *Scholarship Reconsidered: Priorities for the Professoriate*, Carnegie Foundation for the Advancement of Teaching, Princeton, NJ: Princeton University Press.

BROERS, A., FOLLET, B., ROBERTS, D. and SUTHERLAND, S. (1996) 'We are the champions', *The Observer*, 22 December, p. 21.

BROWN, G. (1997) 'Why Labour is still loyal to the poor', Saturday Essay *The Guardian*, 2 August, p. 2.

BROWN, P. and SCASE, R. (1997) 'Universities and employers: Rhetoric and reality', in SMITH, A. and WEBSTER, F. (eds) *The Postmodern University? Contested Visions of Higher Education in Society*, Buckingham: SRHE and Open University Press.

BURGHES, D. (1996) 'Why we lag behind in maths', *Times Educational Supplement*, 15 March, p. 11.

CALLENDER, C. and KEMPSON, E. (1996) *Student Finances. Income, Expenditure and Take-up of Student Loans*, London: Policy Studies Institute.

COATES, D. (1975) *The Labour Party and the Struggle for Socialism*, Cambridge: Cambridge University Press.

COATES, D. (1980) *Labour in Power? A Study of the Labour Government 1974 to 1979*, London: Longman.

COFFIELD, F. and WILLIAMSON, B. (1997) (eds) *Repositioning Higher Education*, Buckingham: SRHE and Open University Press.

COMMITTEE OF ENQUIRY ON RESEARCH IN THE POLYTECHNICS AND COLLEGES SECTOR (1990) *Research in the PCFC Sector — Report of the Committee of Enquiry appointed by the Council*, London: Polytechnic and Colleges Funding Council.

COMMITTEE OF VICE-CHANCELLORS AND PRINCIPALS (1985) *Efficiency in Universities*, (Report of the Steering Committee for Efficiency Studies in Universities 'The Jarratt Report') London: CVCP.

COMMITTEE OF VICE-CHANCELLORS AND PRINCIPALS (1986) *Academic Standards in Universities: Universities Methods and Procedures for Maintaining and Monitoring Academic Standards in the Content and in the Quality of their Teaching*, (The Reynolds Report) London: CVCP.

COMMITTEE OF VICE-CHANCELLORS AND PRINCIPALS (1993) *Promoting People. A Strategic Framework for the Management and Development of Staff in UK Universities*, London: CVCP.

COMMITTEE OF VICE-CHANCELLORS AND PRINCIPALS (1994) *Universities and Communities*, A Report by the Centre for Urban and Regional Development Studies for the CVCP, London: CVCP.

COMMITTEE OF VICE-CHANCELLORS AND PRINCIPALS (1995a) *The Growth in Student Numbers in British Higher Education*, Briefing Note, February, London: CVCP.

COMMITTEE OF VICE-CHANCELLORS AND PRINCIPALS (1995b) *CVCP's Public Expenditure Survey Submission 1995. The Case for Increased Investment in Universities* N/95/99, London: CVCP.

COMMITTEE OF VICE-CHANCELLORS AND PRINCIPALS (1997a) *Higher Education Statistics*, London: CVCP.

COMMITTEE OF VICE-CHANCELLORS AND PRINCIPALS (1997b) *A Summary of the Work of the Admissions Review Steering Group*, London: CVCP.

COMMITTEE OF VICE-CHANCELLORS AND PRINCIPALS (1997c) 'Government's spending announcement for England 1998–99 (FY)', *CVCP Information for Members*, 23 September, 1/97/87.

COMMITTEE OF VICE-CHANCELLORS AND PRINCIPALS (1997d) 'CVCP annual residential conference 1997: Closing communiqué', *CVCP Information for Members*, 19 September, 1/97/83.

COMMITTEE OF VICE-CHANCELLORS AND PRINCIPALS (1997e) *A New Partnership: Universities, Students, Business and the Nation*, London: CVCP.

COMMITTEE ON STANDARDS IN PUBLIC LIFE (1996) *Standards in Public Life — Local Public Spending Bodies*, London: HMSO.

CONFEDERATION OF BRITISH INDUSTRY (1994) *Thinking Ahead; Ensuring the Expansion of Higher Education into the 21st Century*, London: CBI.

COUNCIL FOR INDUSTRY AND HIGHER EDUCATION (1995) *A Wider Spectrum of Opportunities*, London: CIHE.

COUNCIL FOR INDUSTRY AND HIGHER EDUCATION (1996a) *Helping Students Towards Success at Work*, London: CIHE.

References

COUNCIL FOR INDUSTRY AND HIGHER EDUCATION (1996b) *Trends in Higher Education*, November, London: CIHE.

CROSLAND, A. (1965) Speech by Anthony Crosland, Secretary of State for Education and Science at Woolwich Polytechnic, 27 April.

DEARING, R. (1996) *Review of Qualifications for 16–19-year-olds*, Main Report, London: School Curriculum and Assessment Authority.

DEARING, R. (1997) 'Dearing's summary', *Times Higher Education Supplement*, 25 July, p. i.

DEPARTMENT FOR EDUCATION (1994) *Student Numbers in Higher Education — Great Britain 1982/3 to 1992/93*, Statistical Bulletin 13/94, August.

DEPARTMENT FOR EDUCATION AND EMPLOYMENT (1995) *European Year of Lifelong Learning 1996, Criteria for Applications for Funding for Actions Under European Year of Lifelong Learning*, December 1995, London: DfEE.

DEPARTMENT FOR EDUCATION AND EMPLOYMENT (1996) *Departmental Report The Government's Expenditure Plans 1996–97 to 1998–99*, Cmnd 3210, London: HMSO.

DEPARTMENT FOR EDUCATION AND EMPLOYMENT (1997a) *Evidence to Dearing. The Size and Shape of Higher Education*, London: DfEE.

DEPARTMENT FOR EDUCATION AND EMPLOYMENT (1997b) *Higher Education for the 21st Century*, London: HMSO.

DEPARTMENT FOR EDUCATION AND EMPLOYMENT, ANALYTICAL SERVICES HIGHER EDUCATION DIVISION (1997c) *Projections of Demand for Higher Education in Great Britain*, February.

DEPARTMENT OF EDUCATION AND SCIENCE (1967) *Education Statistics for the United Kingdom 1967*, London: HMSO.

DEPARTMENT OF EDUCATION AND SCIENCE (1991) *Student Numbers in Higher Education — Great Britain 1979 to 1989*, Statistical Bulletin 10/91, May.

DEPARTMENT OF EDUCATION AND SCIENCE (1992) *Student Numbers in Higher Education — Great Britain 1980 to 1990*, Statistical Bulletin 8/92, June.

DEPARTMENT OF HEALTH (1997) 'Government's plans for higher education reform strengthen training for NHS Staff — Dobson', Press Release 97/244, 23 September.

DUKE, C. (1997) 'Towards a lifelong curriculum', in COFFIELD, F. and WILLIAMSON, B. (eds) *Repositioning Higher Education*, Buckingham: SRHE and Open University Press.

ELLIOTT, R.F. and DUFFUS, K. (1996) 'What has been happening to pay in the public service section of the British economy?', *British Journal of Industrial Relations*, **34**(1).

ENGINEERING COUNCIL (1997a) *Standards and Routes to Registration — SARTOR*. 3rd Edition 1997, Part 1. An Engineering Policy Document, London: Engineering Council.

ENGINEERING COUNCIL (1997b) *Standards and Routes to Registration SARTOR*, London: Engineering Council.

FIELDHOUSE, R. (1978) *The Workers' Educational Association: Aims and Achievements, 1903–1977*, Syracuse, NY: Syracuse University Publications in Continuing Education.

FIELDHOUSE, R. (1985) 'The problems of objectivity, social purpose and ideological commitment in English university adult education', in TAYLOR, R., ROCKHILL, K. and FIELDHOUSE, R. (eds) *University Adult Education in England and the USA: A Reappraisal of the Liberal Tradition*, London: Croom Helm.

FIELDHOUSE, R. (1996) *A History of Modern British Adult Education*, Leicester: NIACE.

FORTH, E. (1997) 'Clichéd Dearing gets a D for disappointment', *Times Higher Education Supplement*, 22 August, p. 12.

FULTON, O. (1993) 'Institutional strategies for staff renewal', *CRE-action Human Resources at University*, No. 102, pp. 55–64.

FURTHER EDUCATION FUNDING COUNCIL (1996) 'Student numbers, retention, achievements and destinations at colleges in the further education sector in England 1995–96', Press Release.

GIBBONS, M., LIMOGES, C., NOWOTNY, H., SCHWARZMAN, S., SCOTT, P. and TROW, M. (1994) *The New Production of Knowledge: The Dynamics of Science and Research in Contemporary Societies*, London: Sage.

GOSDEN, P. (1976) *Education in the Second World War: A Study in Policy and Administration*, London: Methuen.

GOSDEN, P. (1983) *The Education System Since 1944*, Oxford: Martin Robertson.

HALSEY, A.H. (1993) 'Opening wide the doors of higher education', *Briefings for the Paul Hamlyn Foundation National Commission on Education*, London: Heinemann, pp. 77–88.

HARRIS, M. (1996) *Review of Postgraduate Education* (HEFCE, CVCP and SCOP), Bristol: HEFCE.

HATTERSLEY, R. (1997) 'Why Labour is wrong about income tax', *The Guardian*, 6 August, p. 15.

HAY MANAGEMENT CONSULTANTS (1997) *Independent Pay Commission Report on Pay in Higher Education*, London: Universities and Colleges Employers Association.

HIGHER EDUCATION FUNDING COUNCIL FOR ENGLAND (1993) *Funding for Backlog Maintenance Work in 1993–94 and 1994–95*, Circular 12/93, April, Bristol: HEFCE.

HIGHER EDUCATION FUNDING COUNCIL FOR ENGLAND (1995a) *Report on Quality Assessment 1992–1995* M18/95. Bristol: HEFCE.

HIGHER EDUCATION FUNDING COUNCIL FOR ENGLAND (1995b) *HEFCE Report on Quality Assessment 1992–1995*, Bristol: HEFCE.

HIGHER EDUCATION FUNDING COUNCIL FOR ENGLAND (1995c) *Analysis of 1995 Strategic Plans and Financial Forecasts*, Circular 28/95, Bristol: HEFCE.

HIGHER EDUCATION FUNDING COUNCIL FOR ENGLAND (1996a) *Widening Access to Higher Education*, A Report by the HEFCE's Advisory Group on Access and Participation, M9/96, Bristol: HEFCE.

HIGHER EDUCATION FUNDING COUNCIL FOR ENGLAND (1996b) *Evaluation of the Teaching and Learning Technology Programme*, (by Coopers & Lybrand, Institute of Education and the Tavistock Institute) M21/96, Bristol: HEFCE.

HIGHER EDUCATION FUNDING COUNCIL FOR ENGLAND (1996c) *Recurrent Grant for the Academic Year 1996–97: Final Allocations*, Circular 12/96, Bristol: HEFCE.

HIGHER EDUCATION FUNDING COUNCIL FOR ENGLAND (1996d) *Analysis of 1996 Financial Forecasts*, Circular 15/96, Bristol: HEFCE.

HIGHER EDUCATION FUNDING COUNCIL FOR ENGLAND (1996e) *Institutions' Strategic Plans: Analysis of 1996 Submissions*, Circular 20/96, Bristol: HEFCE.

HIGHER EDUCATION FUNDING COUNCIL FOR ENGLAND (1997) *Report on Quality Assessment 1995–1996*, M1/97, Bristol: HEFCE.

HIGHER EDUCATION QUALITY COUNCIL (1996a) *Code of Practice for Overseas Collaborative Provision in Higher Education*, London: HEQC.

HIGHER EDUCATION QUALITY COUNCIL (1996b) *Inter-institutional Variability of Degree Results: An Analysis in Selected Subjects*, Graduate Standards Programme, London: HEQC.

HIGHER EDUCATION QUALITY COUNCIL (1996c) *Modular Higher Education in the UK in Focus*, London: HEQC.

HIGHER EDUCATION QUALITY COUNCIL (1997) *Graduate Standards Programme Final Report*, London: HEQC.

HIGHER EDUCATION STATISTICS AGENCY (1996) *The Shape and Size of Higher Education in the mid-1990s*, A Report for the National Committee of Inquiry into Higher Education, Cheltenham: HESA.

HIGHER EDUCATION STATISTICS AGENCY (1997) *Students in Higher Education Institutions 1996/97*, Data Report, Cheltenham: HESA.

HILLMAN, J. (1996) *University for Industry: Creating a National Learning Network*, London: Institute for Public Policy Research.

HMSO (1996) *Social Trends 1996*, London: HMSO.

HOLFORD, J. (1994) *Union Education in Britain: A TUC Activity*, Nottingham: University of Nottingham.

HOUSE, D. and WATSON, D. (1995) 'Managing change' in WARNER, D. and CROSTHWAITE, E. (eds) *Human Resource Management in Higher and Further Education*, Buckingham: SRHE and Open University Press.

HUBER, M., GLASSICK, C. and MAEROFF, G. (1997) *Scholarship Assessed: Evaluation of the Professoriate*, Carnegie Foundation for the Advancement of Teaching, San Francisco CA: Jossey-Bass Inc.

INSTITUTE FOR EMPLOYMENT STUDIES (1996) *University Challenge: Student Choices in the 21st Century*, A report to the CVCP, Report Number 306, Brighton: IES.

JEPSON, N. (1973) *The Beginnings of English University Adult Education: Policy and Problems*, London: Michael Joseph.

JOINT PLANNING GROUP FOR QUALITY ASSURANCE IN HIGHER EDUCATION (1996) *Final Report*, December.

KENNEDY, H. (1997) *Learning Works: Widening Participation in Further Education*, Coventry: Further Education Funding Council.

KENWAY, J. et al. (1997) 'Marketing education in the post modern age', *Journal of Education Policy*, **8**(2), pp. 105–22.

KNAPPER, C. and CROPLEY, A. (1991) *Lifelong Learning and Higher Education*, second edition, London: Kogan Page.

LABOUR PARTY (1996) *Lifelong Learning: A Consultation Document*, London: The Labour Party.

LINDOP, N. (1985) *Academic Validation in Public Sector Higher Education*, (Report of the Committee of Enquiry into the Academic Validation of Degree Courses in Public Sector Higher Education), London: HMSO.

LOVETT, T. (1975) *Adult Education, Community Development and the Working Class*, London: Ward Lock Educational.

LOVETT, T. (1988) (ed.) *Radical Approaches to Adult Education: A Reader*, London: Routledge.

MACFARLANE, A. (1992) *Teaching and Learning in an Expanding Higher Education System*, (Report of a Working Party of the Committee of Scottish University Principals), Edinburgh: CSUP.

McILROY, J. (1985) 'Adult education and the role of the client — The TUC education scheme 1929–1980', *Studies in the Education of Adults*, **16**(2).

McILROY, J. (1988) 'Storm and stress: The Trades Union Congress and the university adult education 1964–1974', *Studies in the Education of Adults*, **20**(1).

McNICOLL, I. (1995) *The Impact of the Scottish Higher Education Sector on the Economy of Scotland*, Glasgow: Committee of Scottish Higher Education Principals.

MILIBAND, R. (1969) *The State in Capitalist Society*, London: Weidenfeld and Nicolson.

MILIBAND, R. (1972) *Parliamentary Socialism: A Study in the Politics of Labour*, second edition, London: Merlin Press.

MILIBAND, R. (1994) *Socialism for a Sceptical Age*, Cambridge: Polity Press.

MILLAR, J.P.M. (1979) *The Labour College Movement*, London: NCLC Publishing Society.

MODOOD, T. and SHINER, M. (1994) *Ethnic Minorities and Higher Education. Why Are There Differential Rates of Entry?*, London: Policy Studies Institute.

NATIONAL ACADEMIES POLICY ADVISORY GROUP (1996) *Research Capability of the University System*, London: NAPAG.

NATIONAL ADVISORY COUNCIL FOR EDUCATION AND TRAINING TARGETS (1997) *Skills for 2000* (Report on progress towards the National Targets for Education and Training), London: NACETT.

NATIONAL COMMISSION ON EDUCATION (1993) *Learning to Succeed* (Report of the Paul Hamlyn Foundation National Commission on Education), London: Heinemann.

NATIONAL COMMITTEE OF INQUIRY INTO HIGHER EDUCATION (1997) *Higher Education in the Learning Society* (The Dearing Report) (Summary Report, the Report of the Scottish Committee, and the various appended 'Reports' and 'Appendices').

NATIONAL UNION OF STUDENTS (1996) *Opportunity, Diversity and Partnership — The Student Agenda for Higher Education*, London: NUS.

NCH ACTION FOR CHILDREN (1996) *NCH Action for Children Fact File*, London: NCH.

NIACE (1993) *An Adult Higher Education a Vision: A Policy Discussion Paper*, Leicester: National Institute of Adult Continuing Education.

OSBORNE, P. (1995) 'The politics of time' cited in EAGLETON, T. (1996) *The Illusions of Post-Modernism*, Oxford: Blackwell.

PREST, CASR AND THE UNIVERSITY OF MANCHESTER (1996) *Survey of Research Equipment in UK Universities*, (for CVCP, HEFCE, HEFCW and SHEFC), London: CVCP.

PREST, CASR AND THE UNIVERSITY OF MANCHESTER (1997) *Survey of Teaching Equipment in Higher Education Institutions in England and Wales* (for CVCP, HEFCE, HEFCW and SCOP), Bristol: HEFCE.

QUALITY SUPPORT CENTRE (1995) 'Students in UK higher education', Statistical Supplement, *Higher Education Digest*, Issue 23, autumn, London: QSC.

ROBBINS, L. (1963) *Report of the Committee on Higher Education*, London: HMSO.

ROBERTSON, D. (1994) *Choosing to Change; Extending Access, Choice and Mobility in Higher Education*, (Report of the HEQC CAT Development Project), London: HEQC.

RODERICK, G. and STEPHENS, M. (1982) (eds) *The British Malaise: Industrial Performance, Education and Training in Britain Today*, Barcombe: Falmer Press Ltd.

ROYAL SOCIETY (1995) *Peer Review. An Assessment of Recent Developments*, London: Royal Society.

RUSTIN, M. (1994) 'Flexibility in higher education', in BURROWS, R. and LOADER, B. (eds) *Towards a Post-Fordist Welfare State?*, London and New York: Routledge.

SCOTT, P. (1995) *The Meanings of Mass Higher Education*, Buckingham: SRHE and Open University Press.

SEFTON, T. (1997) *The Changing Distribution of the Social Wage*, London: Suntory and Toyota International Centres for Economics and Related Disciplines.

SILVER, H. (1996) 'External examining in higher education: A secret history', in ALDRICH, R. (ed.) *In History and In Education: Essays Presented to Peter Gordon*, London and Portland OR: Woburn Press, pp. 178–208.

SMITH, A. and WEBSTER, F. (1997) (eds) *The Postmodern University? Contested Visions of Higher Education in Society*, Buckingham: SRHE and Open University Press.

SMITHERS, A. and ROBINSON, P. (1995) *Post-18 Education: Growth, Change, Prospect*, Council for Industry and Higher Education, Executive Briefing, London: CIHE.

TAYLOR, R. (1996) 'Preserving the liberal tradition in "New Times"', in WALLIS, J. (ed.) *Liberal Adult Education: The End of an Era?*, Nottingham: University of Nottingham, Continuing Education Press, pp. 61–75.

TAYLOR, R. (1997) 'The emerging university system and concepts of self-directed learning: A sympathetic critique', Paper for Society for Research into Higher Education Conference, 'Beyond the First Degree', University of Warwick, December 1997.

TAYLOR, R., ROCKHILL, K. and FIELDHOUSE, R. (1985) (eds) *University Adult Education in England and the USA: A Reappraisal of the Liberal Tradition*, London: Croom Helm.

THOMPSON, E.P. (1963) *The Making of the English Working Class*, London: Gollancz.

THOMPSON, E.P. (1965) *Education and Experience*, Albert Mansbridge Memorial Lecture Series, University of Leeds.

THOMPSON, J. (1980) (ed.) *Adult Education for a Change*, London: Hutchinson.

THOMPSON, J. and MAYO, M. (1996) (eds) *Adult Education and Social Change*, Leicester: NIACE.

TUCKETT, A. (1997) *Lifelong Learning in England and Wales: An Overview and Guide to Issues Arising from the European Year of Lifelong Learning*, Leicester: NIACE.

USHER, R., BRYANT, I. and JOHNSTON, R. (1997) *Adult Education and the Postmodern Challenge: Learning Beyond the Limits*, London: Routledge.

WAGNER, L. (1995) 'A thirty-year perspective: From the sixties to the nineties', in SCHULLER, T. (ed.) *The Changing University*, Buckingham: SRHE and Open University Press.

WALDEN, G. (1996) *We Should Know Better: Solving the Education Crisis*, London: Fourth Estate.

WALLIS, J. (1995) (ed.) *Liberal Adult Education: The End of an Era?*, Nottingham: University of Nottingham.

WARD, K. and TAYLOR, R. (1986) (eds) *Adult Education and the Working Class: Education for the Missing Millions*, London: Croom Helm.

WARD, L. (1997) 'How Dearing's members fail to add up', *Independent*, 26 September, p. 8.

WATSON, D. (1996) 'Modularity: For and against', in Higher Education Quality Council *Modular Higher Education in the UK in Focus*, London: HEQC.

WATSON, D. (forthcoming) 'The limits to diversity', in JARY, D. and PARKER, M. (eds) *The Dilemmas of Mass Higher Education: Issues for a Post-Dearing HE System*, Stoke-on-Trent: Staffordshire University Press.

WATSON, D., SCURRY, D., BROOKES, J., LINDSAY, R. and COGHILL, C. (1989) *Managing the Modular Course: Perspectives from Oxford Polytechnic*, Milton Keynes: SRHE and Open University Press.

WEBSTER, F. and ROBINS, K. (1989) *The Technical Fix: Education, Computers and Industry*, London: Macmillan.

WESTWOOD, S. and THOMAS, T. (1991) (eds) *Radical Agendas? The Politics of Adult Education*, Leicester: NIACE.

WINN, S. and STEVENSON, R. (1997) 'Student loans: Are the policy objectives being achieved?', *Higher Education Quarterly*, **51**(2), pp. 144–63.

Index